DEAREST FATHER

DEAREST FATHER

◆

THE CIVIL WAR
LETTERS OF
LT. FRANK DICKERSON,
A SON OF
BELFAST, MAINE

EDITED AND NARRATED BY
H. DRAPER HUNT

North Country Press
Unity, Maine

Library of Congress Cataloging-in-Publication Data

Dickerson, Frank, 1841-1866.
   Dearest father, the Civil War letters of Lt. Frank Dickerson, a
son of Belfast, Maine / edited and narrated by H. Draper Hunt ;
foreword by Gladys Hasty Carroll.
      p.   cm.
   Includes bibliographical references (p.   ) and index.
   ISBN 0-945980-36-1 (trade paper) : $14.95
   1. Dickerson, Frank, 1841-1866—Correspondence.   2. United States—
History—Civil War, 1861-1865—Personal narratives.   3. United States.
Army. Cavalry, 5th.   4. Maine—History—Civil War, 1861-1865—
Personal narratives.   5. Soldiers—Maine—Belfast—Correspondence.
6. Belfast (Me.)—Biography.   I. Hunt, H. Draper (Harry Draper)
II. Title.
   E492.5 5th.D5   1992
   973.7'81'092—dc20   92-28299
                                                                  CIP

© 1992 by North Country Press. All rights reserved.

Book and cover design: Douglas Coffin, Belfast, ME
"Lincoln Letter" cover photograph: Bill Finney, Concord, NH

Indexing: Shirley Landmesser, Searsport, ME
Composition: Typeworks, Belfast, ME
Manufactured in the United States of America

The Publishers acknowledge with appreciation the special and often
personal contributions, as well as encouragement, made in connection with
this Work by many people, among them those professionally involved in it.
They include:

Diane Barnes, Carl Becker, Carol Bisbee, June Brown, Lance Brown,
Stan Brown, Read Brugger, John and Hanna Burleigh, John G. Dickerson, Jr.,
Charlene Farris, Jenny Ferguson, Bill Finney, Steve Goguen, Doris Hall,
Andrew Kuby, Andy Lacher, Shirley Landmesser, Michele Leach, P.A. Lenk,
Isabel Maresh, Donald Mortland, Gloria Oliver, Delores Page, Joyce Page,
Phil Rackliffe, Katrina Richardson, Lucy Richardson, Hugh McLellan Russell,
Morris Slugg, Kathleen Whalin, Bill and Cindy White.

10 9 8 7 6 5 4 3 2 1

FOREWORD

There is a headstone, in an old cemetery atop a hill in Belfast, Maine, overlooking Penobscot Bay, that marks the grave of Frank W. Dickerson, a native son who,with conviction and idealism, in 1862 went to fight with the Union in the War that was to pit brother against brother for five awful years.

Today, some 130 years later, although no photograph of Frank is known to exist, we have 77 letters penned in a graceful hand to his father, Jonathan, back in Belfast.

Through these letters, which come to us from the collection of my dear friend, Lucy Burleigh Richardson, we are able to frame a picture of this gallant young soldier in our imagination. The accompanying narration prepared by Civil War scholar H. Draper Hunt of the University of Southern Maine provides graphic insight into not only Frank's letters, but the War at the time. Moreover, Dr. Hunt's accounting of events in Belfast is particularly revealing of the mood on the home front.

The letters reveal a young man who went to war because it was the right thing to do. Frank participated in twelve major battles; he was injured; he had his horse shot out from under him; he was acquainted with John Wilkes Booth and so suffered a special agony over the tragedy that took Lincoln from the nation. Ultimately, he suffered a debilitating illness and, no longer able to fight, served out his remaining time fulfilling behind-the-lines support responsibilities as best he could. And, oh, how toward the end he longed to come home to his family!

But he never saw Belfast again. His race with death ended aboard a steamer in Boston Harbor on February 17, 1866, when, at the age of 24, Frank Dickerson died in his father's arms. Finally, he could come home, to rest forever on the hill in the little city by the Bay.

I have said frequently that life is more precious to me than literature, and that I write—and read—only out of eagerness for further clarification of what I see and hear and feel. In these letters, aided by the clarity and power of Draper Hunt's stirring narration, I see and hear and feel through the eyes and ears and heart of Frank Dickerson. For that experience, I am grateful.

Gladys Hasty Carroll

South Berwick, Maine

DEDICATION

In memory of our forebears,
especially our magnificent Grandmother,
Lucy Dickerson Burleigh,
referred to as "LuLu" in the letters.

With love for Gary and his family, Trina, Justin and Sarah.

For Jean Boston, my sister.

For John Burleigh, my brother.

We remember so many years ago
our youthful gales of laughter
when John inherited Great-Uncle Frank's sword!

And always, always, for Dwight,
who endured my asking for the 1,000th time,
"What do you think that word is?"

Lucy Burleigh Richardson
Amherst, New Hampshire, 1992

DEDICATION II

For Lucy Richardson,
who reveres, and has kept alive,
the memory of
Frank Wilberforce Dickerson, her grandmother
Lucy Dickerson Burleigh's half-brother.

—H.Draper Hunt
Portland, Maine
Summer, 1992

CONTENTS

PREFACE

These are the Civil War letters of Frank Wilberforce Dickerson of Belfast, Maine, successively second and first lieutenant and, posthumously, brevet captain and brevet major, 5th U.S. Cavalry. Transcribed with care and love from their original graceful old script by his great-niece, Lucy Richardson, they reveal a gallant young officer, deeply devoted to the Union cause and to his family, fighting bravely in every engagement in which he took part. Wounded at the furious cavalry battle of Brandy Station (June, 1863), Frank could no longer sustain a combat role and served in a series of detached services until his tragically premature death from disease in February 1866.

Although Frank entered the service the spring of 1862, the bulk of his letters fall in 1864 and 1865. Regrettably, if Frank penned any battlefield descriptions (and in addition to numerous cavalry skirmishes, he took part in the mammoth battles of Antietam and Fredericksburg), none but a fragmentary description of the aftermath of Antietam has survived.

Thus I've written a narrative history of the Civil War which, although far from comprehensive, provides the background and setting for Lieutenant Dickerson's career and furnishes substantial descriptions of battles he experienced but didn't describe in the extant letters. The narrative also bridges the letters from first to last.

A word on editorial method. I have silently corrected obvious spelling errors and silently inserted commas here and there for greater clarity and ease of reading. The obtrusive *[sic]* to denote the letter-writer's, not the editor's, errors, has been kept to a bare minimum. Occasionally a word has been inserted in brackets where I felt Frank omitted said word. Otherwise the letters are exactly as he wrote them.

—*H. Draper Hunt*

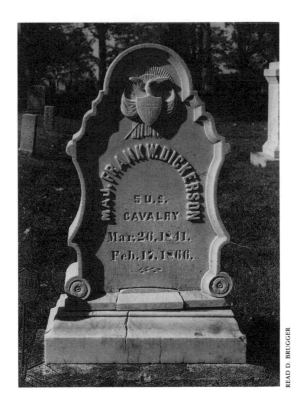

"And the War Came"

THE OLD MAN HATED Yankees, "The perfidious, malignant & vile Yankee race", as he put it.[1] So it was with a feeling of grim pleasure that Edmund Ruffin, agricultural authority, slave owner and Virginian secessionist pulled the lanyard of a massive 64-pound Columbiad that sent a shell plowing into the northeast parapet of Fort Sumter at the entrance to the harbor of Charleston, South Carolina. Captain Abner Doubleday, awakened in the Fort by the impact of the missile, reckoned that it was "the one that probably came with Mr. Ruffin's compliments". Then, all around the harbor, Southern guns opened up on Sumter, which returned fire ineffectively after a two-hour delay. It was April 12, 1861. Two days later, Sumter's garrison abandoned the battered fort, and Ruffin and his Palmetto Guard Comrades entered the fort, which now flew the Stars and Bars of the Confederate States of America and the distinctive Palmetto flag of South Carolina. The old man, his long white hair streaming to his shoulders, picked up shell fragments as souvenirs, then returned to Charleston, the unlikely first hero of the Civil War![2]

Four years later, President Abraham Lincoln stood in a shaft of sudden sunlight at his second Inauguration and observed:

> On the occasion corresponding to this four years ago, all thoughts were anxiously directed to an impending civil war. All dreaded it—all sought to avert it. While the inaugural address was being delivered from this place, devoted altogether to *saving* the Union without war, insurgent agents were in the city seeking to *destroy* it without war—seeking to dissol[v]e the

Union, and divide effects, by negotiation. Both parties deprecated war; but one of them would *make* war rather than let the nation survive; and the other would *accept* war rather than let it perish. And the war came.[3]

"The Civil War is, for the American imagination, the great single event of our history", Robert Penn Warren wrote. "Without too much wrenching, it may, in fact, be said to *be* American history."[4] By whatever name men and women called it—the Civil War, the War Between the States, the Brothers' War, the War to Suppress Yankee Arrogance or, simply, The War—it was the great single fact in the lives of mid-nineteenth century Americans. And when it began on that dark April morning in Charleston, few could have foretold its incredible scope and tenacity and its myriad and matchless horrors. Americans reacted to the attack on Fort Sumter with a kind of relief, a liberation from a decade of wrangling between North and South over slavery expansion and the ultimate fate of this "peculiar institution". At the news from Charleston, a woman leaped up in the Ohio Senate Gallery and shrieked, "Glory to God!" Americans North and South seemed drunk on nationalistic fervor. The *Chicago Tribune* trumpeted

There is a republic! the gates of Janus are open; the storm is upon us. Let the cry be, The Sword of the Lord and of Gideon! From this hour let no Northern man or woman tolerate in his or her presence the utterance of a word of treason. We say to the Tories and lickspittles in the community, a patient and reluctant, but at last an outraged and maddened people will no longer endure your hissing. You must keep your venom sealed or go down.

A western Methodist bishop reported exultantly

There has been held a great Union Convention. . . . It was held amid the fortresses of the everlasting hills. The Rocky Mountains presided, the mighty Mississippi made the motion, the Allegheny Mountains seconded it and every mountain and hill, valley and plain, in this vast country, sent up a unanimous voice; Resolved, that we are one and inseparable and what God has joined together, let no man put asunder.

A fiery Boston clergyman, whose worried mother asked, "Has God sent you to preach the sword, or to preach Christ?" replied, "Dear mother. God has sent me not only to preach the sword but to *use* it. When this Government tumbles, look amongst the ruins for . . . Your Star-Spangled Banner Son."[5]

A Georgia boy crowed, "The first time I heard Dixie, I felt like I could take a cornstalk, get on the Mason and Dixon's line and whip the whole Yankee Nation."[6]

Behind such militancy lay ignorance and false assumptions: that the war would be short, virtually bloodless and a glorious Union or Confederate victory, depending on one's residence and loyalties.

The Civil War cost 623,026 lives, some lost in 10,455 military actions, large and small, and the others through disease. Hundreds of thousands more were wounded. These are the grimmest statistics in a war which eventually cost the Union $2,500,000 a day and a total Federal expenditure on strictly war costs of $3,027,791,000.[7] The Confederacy paid an even higher monetary price, since added to its heavy war expenditures must be hundreds of millions represented by heavy destruction of Southern property and the expropriation, without recompense, of 3.5 million slaves worth several billion dollars.

But these grim realities lay hidden, mercifully and tragically, from the young men of 1861, as they descended on incredibly crowded recruiting offices. Young plowboys flocked in from their fields (the typical Civil War soldier was a farmer between 18 and 29), young mechanics left their shops and clerks their counting houses to answer the beguiling call to arms. To most young men in April, 1861, the banners snapping in the breeze, the pretty girls with their kisses and fluttering handkerchiefs, the politicians with their high-sounding patriotic phrases and the bands playing stirring military airs all combined to make war carnival and picnic. And so it seemed, as well, to the young patriots of Belfast, Maine.

A view of Belfast, Maine from the "East Side," circa 1860. The steeple of the Unitarian Church with its historic clock is visible to the right of center. (Reprinted courtesy of the Belfast Free Library)

CHAPTER I

Frank Dickerson Goes to War

THEY EXPECTED JUDGE Jonathan Garland Dickerson, Belfast's noted orator, to speak, and he didn't disappoint them. Dickerson's stirring patriotic paean to the indissoluble Union was delivered in Peirce's Hall on April 19 to an enthusiastic crowd already excited by the news from Fort Sumter and President Abraham Lincoln's call for 75,000 ninety-day volunteers to crush the rebellion. All over town, American flags snapped in the breeze— from stores, workshops, political party headquarters, the post office and the customhouse, as Belfasters proclaimed their loyalty to the United States.[1]

The bustling little city on the Passagassawakeag River nestled among hills rolling down to the shores of Penobscot Bay. Many residents went down to the sea in ships or built them; others marketed farm products from the surrounding countryside, buying from wagons streaming into town on market days and shipping by sea. Still others sold goods and services ranging from pork, to bread, to haircuts to their fellow-citizens.

"Peace and prosperity reigned on every hand, the law breakers were few, no frowning policemen, with comical Kaiser helmets, paraded the streets, and such was the general character of the citizens, that they and their home might well have furnished the poet a fit subject for an Arcadian song."[2]

And then the war came.

"Never in the history of your country has there been anything like the spirit aroused by the virtual declaration of war on the part of the Confederate States," the *Belfast Republican Journal* proclaimed. And it was altogether fitting and proper that Judge

5

Dickerson should play a leading role in Belfast's patriotic response, as the town's two banks pledged one-quarter of their capital to the State of Maine as a war loan, and the city appropriated $5,000 to help the families of volunteers. Dickerson had long been a community leader and a prominent Democrat.[3]

Jonathan Garland Dickerson was born in New Chester, New Hampshire on November 5, 1811. Educated at New Hampton Institute, where he honed debating skills, and at Waterville (now Colby) College, he received his bachelor's degree in 1836, then studied law. In 1839, he was admitted to the Maine Bar and hung out his shingle in Prospect (later Searsport), the town bordering Belfast. After an 1842 term in the Maine Legislature representing Prospect, he served as Deputy Collector of Customs in Frankfort, Maine, and in 1849, moved to Belfast. Six years later, he bought the *Belfast Republican Journal* and operated it for three years.[4] Twice county attorney, he won the prized collectorship of the Port of Belfast, appointed by Democratic President James Buchanan in 1858. Dickerson eventually converted to the new Republican Party and was rewarded by a seat on the Maine Supreme Judicial Court in 1862, with reappointment in 1869 and 1876.

Joseph Williamson reports glowingly that Associate Justice Dickerson's "professional life of nearly forty years was characterized by untiring industry, sturdy honesty, and great independence of character. He was regarded as a wise and safe counselor, an eloquent and earnest advocate, and as judge, learned and able, bringing to the investigation of legal questions keen powers of research and analysis, making his decisions from principle rather than from precedent. His written opinions, prepared with scrupulous care, were models of their kind."[5]

This Belfast first citizen won fame, too, for his oratorical prowess. While still living in West Prospect he delivered the July 4, 1840, oration, and again in 1844. In June, 1844, Dickerson dedicated the meeting place of the Belfast Democratic Association above the Furber & Blair store on Main Street. An American flag floated before this Democratic bastion, which was emblazoned with signs capable of illumination reading "Democratic Hall" and

Peirce's Hall, or Parlor, outside of which Judge Dickerson and other orators often spoke. It was built in 1852. The Unitarian Church steeple is visible at upper right. (Collection of Doris Hall)

A formal portrait of Judge Jonathan Dickerson. His signature appears below it. (Courtesy Waldo County Law Library)

MICHELE LEACH

7

"[James K.] Polk and [George M.] Dallas," the latter honoring the Democracy's Presidential and Vice-Presidential standard-bearers.[6] A decade later, on July 4, artillery thundered, bells rang, a parade escorted by Hydrant Company No. 2 and featuring the Belfast Sax-horn band and a floral cart carrying a "bevy of little girls arrayed in white, each one representing a State in the Union" marched through town and, to no one's surprise, J. G. Dickerson read the Declaration of Independence in the Unitarian Church.[7]

Joy and sorrow punctuated Jonathan Garland Dickerson's life. His first wife, Ellen Louise Getchell, of Waterville married Dickerson on February 13, 1840, bore him a son, Frank Wilberforce Dickerson, and died November 3, 1843. Dickerson married Lydia Jane Merithew of Prospect December 4, 1844. They had two daughters, Ellen Louise and Lucy Ames, and a son, Jeremiah Merithew, all of whom survived their mother, who died of consumption on September 29, 1856 after a long illness "which was borne without a murmur, and whose extremest pains did not withdraw her attention from the interests and well being of her friends, husband and children." Two years later on March 21, 1858, tragedy struck again when little Jerrie Dickerson died of "accidental burning by fluid" at the age of 7 years, 5 months.[8]

The 1860 Belfast census reveals that Judge Dickerson, age 48 and "Council-at-law," with real estate valued at $2,500 and personal property at $1,000, had living with him his third wife, Eliza A. [Berry], son Frank W., age 19 and a student, Ellen L., age 13 and little Lucy A., age 5.[9]

What little we know about Frank Dickerson, the oldest son of the family, we glean from his Civil War letters. We learn of his birth on March 26, 1841, know that he attended Belfast schools and Westbrook Seminary (now College) in Westbrook, Maine.[10] If he looked like his distinguished father, he must have been a handsome young man, with chiseled features, although probably not the beard that encircled Judge Dickerson's jaws and firm chin. Apparently when the war came, Frank's preferred service was the U. S. Navy, "and for several months had reason to believe that his wishes would be gratified; but the door of hope in this field of duty was finally closed against him."[11] Perhaps Judge Dickerson's political influence helped his son obtain a commission in the U.S. Cavalry. But young Frank must have felt as did Willard Glazier, 2nd New York Cavalry, who wrote to his sister:

> When our country is threatened with destruction by base and designing men . . . it becomes her sons to go to her rescue and avert the impending ruin. The rebelling South has yet to learn the difference between the true *principles* of the Constitution, and the *delusion* of State rights! . . . I shall return to my studies as soon as the Rebellion is put down and the authority of our Government fully restored, and not until then.[12]

And so, in March 1862, newly minted 2nd Lt. Frank W. Dickerson, 5th U.S. Cavalry, went to war.

CHAPTER II

1862:
Lieutenant Dickerson at War

WHEN LIEUTENANT FRANK DICKERSON rode off to battle, the war had been going on for nearly a year. To paraphrase Winston Churchill, the spring of 1862 was not the end, nor the beginning of the end, but perhaps the end of the beginning.

Frank had missed the "picture-book" phase, when recruits worried not about death or wounds but simply missing the one great battle which would wind the whole thing up. One underage boy, desperate to enroll but raised not to lie, scribbled the number "18" on a scrap of paper, placed it in his shoe and, poker-faced, assured the skeptical recruiter that he was "over eighteen."

"Billy Yanks" and "Johnny Rebs" both woefully underestimated the fighting power and tenacity of their enemy. Northern soldiers, convinced that Southerners were bragging cowards fit only to whip cringing slaves, had no doubt who would win. Rebs boasted that one Southern boy could whip two or five (depending on how free the liquor flowed!) pasty-faced Yankee money-grubbers. One of the tragedies of the Civil War is the degree to which each side underestimated the fighting ability of the other. It took the Seven Days, Antietam, Fredericksburg and a host of other bloody battles to prove that Northern and Southern courage were indistinguishable.

Frank Dickerson had little time to spare pondering Union war aims. What he fought for was, in fact, clear enough in his letters—the flag of the sacred Union, one nation indivisible, North and South, East and West, bound together forever from Maine to California. He sensed that the American way of life

Frank Dickerson's Commission as a Second Lieutenant, dated February 19, 1862, and signed by President Abraham Lincoln and Secretary of War Edwin M. Stanton. Dickerson's Commission as First Lieutenant, also signed by Lincoln and Stanton, was dated July 17, 1862. (Courtesy Colby College Special Collections)

11

could not survive Confederate independence. For then there would be two nations and perhaps, in the future, three or more. So Frank Dickerson fought gallantly to preserve the Union and all that that concept meant in terms of democracy and majority rule. And beginning in 1863, he fought to destroy slavery, although he would have been among the first to admit that this goal of liberation would have impelled few Union men into battle in 1861.

Frank missed the tumultuous, clumsy, greenhorn first phase of the Civil War, when States sent more recruits than could initially be armed and uniformed, when some cavalry and infantry regiments were raised by local worthies too old or fat to ride a horse or totally innocent of the simplest rudiments of drill or parade, much less battlefield, maneuver. America's wars have historically been fought with volunteers, with the Civil War the classic example. Raw recruits had to be whipped into disciplined troops, much against their will, especially as concerned military courtesy and such regular army nonsense, as the boys saw it. As one Indiana soldier put it, "We had enlisted to put down the rebellion and had no patience with the red-tape tom-foolery of the regular service. Furthermore, our boys recognized no superiors except in the line of legitimate duty. Shoulder straps waived, a private was ready at the drop of a hat to thrash his commander; a feat that occurred more than once."[1] Election of junior officers by the men in both Union and Confederate armies compounded the problem; indeed those candidates offering lax discipline regularly won coveted lieutenant's and captain's bars. But regular army officers, and many talented volunteer officers like Joshua Chamberlain of Maine, proved adept at turning citizens into soldiers. One resourceful officer found that his farm-boy recruits couldn't tell left from right. He had each man tie a swatch of hay to his left, and one of straw to his right foot, then bawled out the marching order, "Hay foot! Straw foot!" Gradually, with countless hours of drill, and battlefield experience, grass-green troops ripened into seasoned veterans.[2]

Frank missed the first big battle of the war, which, as President Lincoln observed, pitted greenhorn against greenhorn. Lincoln's primary war challenge was to identify and promote commanders of ability and energy until he found an organizer of Union victory. Alas, Brevet-Lt. Gen. Winfield Scott, 74 years old when the war began, was not that elusive military savior. A lion's heart beat in his huge, arthritic body, always clad in full dress uniform, but he could no longer mount a horse and had to turn battlefield command over to younger men. Brig. Gen. Irvin McDowell was the first. The General was noted for the basket-shaped bamboo hat he wore on the battlefield and for his gluttony at table, where he was known to eat a huge meal and then polish off an entire watermelon for desert.[3]

Brave and well-intentioned but unlucky, McDowell came a cropper on the banks of Bull Run, Virginia, on July 21, 1861. The day began well for the Union but ended in a rout—"Yankee's run" as the Confederates jeered—with the carriages of civilian spectators clogging the roads (a New York Congressman ended up in a Richmond prison temporarily) and adding greatly to the confusion. Out of this early debacle emerged both a greater Union determination than ever to prevail, and 34-year-old Maj. Gen. George B. McClellan—"Little Mac" to his adoring troops—who was Frank Dickerson's first army commander. A fine military figure of a man given to Napoleonic poses when photographed, McClellan had turned in a brilliant record at West Point, the Mexican War and in the peacetime army. A railroad executive when the war began, he won military laurels in western Virginia, attracting President Lincoln's favorable attention.

Appointed to command the military remnants of the Bull Run (First Manassas) battle, reinforced by thousands of new recruits streaming in from all over the North, Little Mac created the Army of the Potomac, second to none in American history. He had splendid rank-and-file material to work with but had to eliminate incompetent officers of the kind described by a volunteer in the 75th New York:

> Tonight not 200 men are in camp. Capt. Catlin, Capt. Hulburt, Lt. Cooper and one or two other officers are under arrest. A hundred more are at houses of ill fame, and the balance are everywhere . . . Col. Alford is very drunk all the time now.[4]

While Frank may have heard of the colonel of the 19th Maine Regiment perambulating surrounding regiments selling discount pies,[5] such officers were quickly weeded out by the General's military boards when the young officer from Belfast joined the Army of the Potomac in the spring of 1862. Both officers and men glowed with discipline and confidence. As McClellan galloped down their ranks, waving his kepi and trailing his glittering staff, his men cheered like demons, convinced they had the finest general, and were part of the finest army, on the planet.

McClellan combined great strengths with serious weaknesses. No other Civil War general could match him as an organizer, disciplinarian and inspirer of troops. But he distrusted politicians, including Commander-in-Chief Lincoln, and rarely confided his plans to the President unless under pressure.

At first fondly amused by his Chief, he came to despise him, referring to Lincoln as "nothing more than a well-meaning baboon" and "the original gorilla."[6] And he always labored under an almost pathological fear that the enemy vastly outnumbered his army, which always made him hesitate to hit the enemy with everything he had. He brooded for months about the huge Confederate army looming across the Potomac River, but when he finally moved against it in March, 1862 (the very month Frank entered the service) he found that army had not only retreated but had defended itself with "Quaker guns" made of painted logs and had been much smaller than the Army of the Potomac all along.

When Frank Dickerson joined the 5th U.S. Cavalry as an element of this great army, he might have snatched a few moments from his military labors to learn something of the history of the cavalry arm in U.S. military service. Cavalry had performed well during the Revolution, particularly the body of horsemen commanded by "Light Horse Harry" Lee, a dashing Virginian and the father of Confederate General Robert E. Lee. But after a brief reappearance in the War of 1812, the cavalry had disappeared from the U.S. Army from 1815 to 1833, the great expense of raising and equipping a cavalry regiment being a major deterrent. In 1855, Secretary of War Jefferson Davis had supplemented

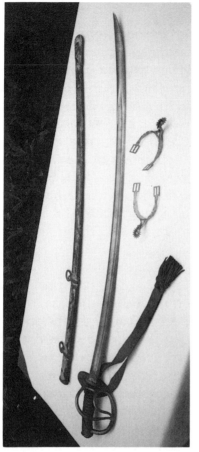

Left: Dickerson's .50-cal. Smith Cavalry Carbine, #4126. The break-breech, percussion carbine, patented June 23, 1857, was manufactured by American Machine Works, Springfield, Mass. (Courtesy John D. Dickerson, Jr). Above: His sword, its scabbard, and his spurs. (Courtesy John and Hanna Burleigh)

America's meager cavalry with two new regiments, the 1st and 2nd U.S. Cavalry. The initial officer roster of the 2nd U.S. boasted a veritable galaxy of future Civil War stars: its Colonel, Albert Sidney Johnston, became a full Confederate general and added a fatal quantity of his own blood to the gory Shiloh battlefield in April, 1862. Robert E. Lee served as lieutenant-colonel, with future Confederate Lt. Gen. William J. Hardee as major, the second major being George H. Thomas, Union major-general and the legendary "Rock of Chickamauga." Captains included future Rebel generals Earl Van Dorn (shot dead by an outraged husband), and Edmund Kirby Smith and future U.S. Cavalry Corps commander George Stoneman. The 2nd U.S. Cavalry, renumbered the 5th U.S. by Act of Congress in August, 1861, became Frank Dickerson's regiment.[7]

"That a non-West Point graduate would receive a commission in a Regular Army unit would not be uncommon in a wartime situation," writes John J. Slonaker, Chief, Historical Reference Branch, U.S. Army Military History Institute.[8] Had Frank Dickerson attended the U.S. Military Academy, he would have been taught that the primary role of the cavalry in war was to carry out thundering charges against enemy infantry as in the days of Napoleon. The French Emperor's cavalry had gained immortality, especially the huge, heavily-armed and padded *cuirassiers*, who, as many as 12,000 strong, smashed into enemy infantry with devastating effect. But U.S. cavalry units served primarily scattered across the western frontier, where the Indians refused to cooperate by massing together to be bowled over by sabre-wielding horsemen, too few in number in any event.

A factor few cavalry experts considered at the outset of the Civil War was that, as Stephen Starr puts it, "dramatic improvement in the firepower in the thirty years preceding the Civil War might . . . have made the traditional cavalry charge a deadly anachronism." The short-ranged, inaccurate Napoleonic smooth-bore musket had given way to the long-range, lethally-accurate rifled musket by 1861. Only a fool would charge massed infantry so armed. Other factors, too, compelled rethinking of the cavalry's role in war.

It was suspected in 1861 that the broken wooded terrain of Virginia would dictate major departures from European cavalry practice, but there was no theorist to predict the nature and extent of these departures nor, until the war was already in its third year did anyone come forward to propose workable alternatives to a doctrine that was equally inapplicable to modern conditions of weaponry and to the special conditions, both human and topographic, of the American Civil War.[9]

Above all others, General McClellan should have been sensitive to, and imaginative in handling, the new cavalry imperatives. He had published *Regulations and Instructions for the Field Service of the United States Cavalry in Time of War* (1861) and had invented the McClellan saddle, standard cavalry issue from then on. While he did acknowledge that "The nature of cavalry service in the United States being quite different from that performed by any in Europe, we ought not to follow blindly any one system but should endeavor to select the good features and engraft them upon a system of our own," he had neglected to forge a powerful, unified, cavalry corps capable of devastating raids into enemy country, which proved so effective later in the war. Admittedly, his manual had stressed guard duty and prevention of surprise attack as the cavalry's primary function, and he stressed the latter duty in orders issued shortly after assuming army command. Like a farmer sowing corn, he scattered his cavalry regiments throughout the Army of the Potomac until they became essentially infantry appendages. A volunteer trooper in McClellan's army reminisced that early in the war "the cavalry were for the most part scattered about and used as escorts, strikers, dog-robbers and orderlies for all the generals and their numerous staff officers from the highest in rank down to the second lieutenants."[10]

The cavalry formed part of the vast and splendid Army of the Potomac which embarked on its first campaign in March, 1862. General McClellan had assembled over 100,000 men, with thousands of wagons, horses, mules, a huge artillery train and support facilities of all kinds and, with matchless efficiency, transported them all by water to the peninsula between Virginia's James and

York Rivers. Their objective: Richmond, capital of the Confederacy. But McClellan had a bad case of what Lincoln called "the slows" all during this crucial campaign. First, he allowed a small Confederate force defending Yorktown on the lower Peninsula to bamboozle him. He lost the month of April preparing an elaborate siege, and just when the giant guns were emplaced to pulverize the enemy, the Rebels quietly abandoned Yorktown. General McClellan crowed triumphantly about his bloodless victory while the Confederates took full advantage of their breathing spell to rush troops from the Department of Northern Virginia to oppose his march. Little Mac outnumbered the Rebels nearly two to one but constantly demanded reinforcements as he closed in on Richmond. Within the sound of its church bells, he successfully beat back poorly coordinated attacks at Fair Oaks and Seven Pines (May 31). Wounded Confederate General Joseph E. Johnston made way for General Robert E. Lee as commander of the Army of Northern Virginia in the most fateful change of command in the entire war. A brilliant, inspiring commander with a full measure of the jugular instinct McClellan lacked, Lee struck a series of savage blows at the Union Army in the Seven Days Battles (June 25-July 1).

Frank Dickerson had joined his company of the 5th U.S. Cavalry on April 15, 1862, at Warwick Court House, and participated in the Yorktown seige and the battle of Williamsburg, as well as virtually daily skirmishes as the Army of the Potomac closed in on Richmond. He distinguished himself at the battle of Hanover Court House (May 27) where, as the historian of the 5th U.S. put it, "his coolness under fire, skill in handling his company, and impetuosity in the attack at once established his character as a soldier."[11]

Now, as the attacks by Lee's Army of northern Virginia forced McClellan into a skillful strategic withdrawal and change of base from White House on the Pamunkey River to Harrison's Landing on the James, Lieutenant Dickerson arrived at corps commander General Fitz-John Porter's headquarters on the battlefront. Informed that a retreat had been ordered, Frank rode back to warn the Cavalry Division and its commander, Brig. Gen.

George Stoneman. He galloped over terrain soon captured by the Confederates, so his mission carried considerable risk. Immediately the alerted horsemen set out for Harrison's Landing and its protective gun- boats and arrived safely. "It was to Lieutenant Dickerson's vigilance and promptness in a great degree that General Stoneman attributed his ability to rescue his command from the victorious enemy."[12]

The last battle of the Seven Days, a rear-guard action at Malvern Hill, saw thousands of Confederate troops charging uphill into the teeth of massed Federal artillery and infantry. The result: a massacre, which covered the green grass before the guns with a blanket of dead and dying Rebels, a horrible, undulating blanket of gray and red. Seven Days casualties: Federal, nearly 16,000, with 1734 killed; Confederate; 20,000, with 3,286 killed.[13]

Frank's first letter, dated August 30, 1862 "On Board Steamer Golden Gate," finds him returning to the Virginia front to rejoin his regiment. He had been in Belfast on sick leave:

Dear Father,

I arrived in Washington last Wednesday night, stopping a day in Portland and also a day in Boston. Had a pleasant journey. On Thursday morning I went down to Alexandria and from there rode up to Gen'l McClellan's Head Quarters about 2 miles distant. Saw Gen'l Williams (to whom I report to duty) Gen'l McClellan's adjt. Gen'l. He told me that our reg't was at Yorktown, but said he would put me on duty at H'd Qut's. as they would be there soon, if I wished, or, I could go to my reg't. I told him that I hadn't entirely recovered from my illness and he said that the trip might do me good. I concluded I should prefer to be with my reg't so went back to Alexandria and got an order for transportation on the first steamer down to Fortress Monroe. The rest of the day I passed up to Washington as well as most all day yesterday (Friday). We left Alexandria at six o'clock last evening on the steamer the Golden Gate. Three other *officers besides myself have the boat all to ourselves, and I have enjoyed the trip so far very much. One of my companions is on Gen'l Keyes' staff, one a Cap't in a R.I. Reg't, and the other Lieutenant in a N.Y. Reg't, all young men. The boat ran last night till about 10 o'clock when she came to anchor till 5 this morning. She has good accomodations which we enjoy to ourselves very much. She goes to the Fortress to carry us down and has no freight on board, but, will probably bring back troops either from the Fortress or Yorktown. We expect to arrive at the Fortress about eight this evening where we shall stop all night and go up to Yorktown in this or some other steamer tomorrow or next day. I am going to take it easy, (being on the salt water agrees with me), Gen'l Williams intimated as much, said I might possibly pass the reg't coming up on my way down but I could go there, and, if I didn't find them, could come back again and join them at Alexandria; in that event, I have quite a little excursion on the water before me. It is [as] cool and comfortable on the boat today as one could wish, though Thursday and Friday which I passed in Washington were exceedingly hot days. My health is better, I think without a doubt, than it was when I left home. I have run around considerably since I left home and have been somewhat tired and heated at times, still I have had no return of the diarrhea and haven't taken my medicine since leaving home. My bowels are quite regular now and I feel stronger than I did the day I left home. I saw Gov. Anderson's family in Washington, took tea there one night, the Gov. himself is away, out west, in Kansas, but is expected back soon when he and Mrs. Anderson think of making a visit down to Maine. Joe is not on Gen'l McDowell's staff but has a $1400.00 clerkship in one of the Depts. I also saw in Washington your friend, Mr. Fuller.[14] I did not do anything with that certificate which I took along with me[15]—I do not desire to be away from my reg't in a time like this when every man no matter*

The U.S. Custom House and Post Office in Belfast. The building was erected in 1855. The Unitarian Church is at left. (Courtesy Waldo County Register of Deeds)

how small his rank ought to be, if he is possibly able, at his post. The country needs the services of all its sons more now than it ever has before and I regard the present as the most critical part of the war. Washington never was in more danger than it is now. The gov't is putting strong garrisons in all the forts around Alexandria and preparing now for its defense. The boat rocks and jars so it is with a great deal of difficulty I have managed to write this letter and I think it will cause even more difficulty to read it than it has me to write it. My love to Mother, Ellen, and Lulu and accept much for yourself from

Your Affec. son Frank

P.S. I got me one of the "aromatic belts or soldiers life preserver" in Boston and think quite well of it. It is made

21

of flannel inside of which there are placed some aromatic
stimulants such as cayenne etc., it completely protects the
stomach, keeping it warm etc. all the time. When you
write direct as follows
  Averill's Brigade
  Army of the Potomac
  Washington, D.C.
Write Soon. I will write again after I find my reg't.

Frank's letter coincided with the Federal debacle at Second Manassas (Bull Run) August 29-30, and he correctly stressed Washington's danger.

General John Pope had breezed into Virginia fresh from modest Western victories to command the new Army of Virginia, made up of elements of other Eastern outfits. A stout, arrogant man, he boasted that his headquarters would be in the saddle, causing Lincoln to wonder where his *hindquarters* would be! And he threatened Confederate civilians with dire punishment if they aided the Rebel war effort. General Lee reacted contemptuously that Pope must be "suppressed," a term he applied to no other Union general. Maj. Gen. Thomas Jonathan ("Stonewall") Jackson set out toward Manassas to begin the process of suppressing Pope. General Lee shortly joined him with the remainder of the Army of Northern Virginia. In a furious two-day battle, Lee, Jackson and Gen. James Longstreet drubbed Pope. One notable campaign casualty was one-armed Brig. Gen. Phil Kearney, who rode through teeming rain and flashes of lightning, clutching his sabre in his only hand and his reins clenched between his teeth, into Confederate lines and a fatal bullet. Having suffered some 16,000 (20 percent) casualties to some 9,000 (19 percent) for the Rebels, the Union army staggered into the Washington defenses, in a grim reprise of First Manassas.

Having thrashed Pope, the Army of Northern Virginia now moved North and invaded Maryland, hoping to win foreign recognition by a victory on enemy soil, to further demoralize the North, and to summon Confederate sympathizers in the state to the Southern colors.

McClellan had been ordered off the peninsula and had rendered minimal assistance (some said deliberately) to the harried Pope. Now, reluctantly restored to full command in Virginia by President Lincoln, General McClellan set out in pursuit with an army of some 80,000 men.

Demonstrating once again his characteristic daring, General Lee divided his army, only half as large as McClellan's, into two major contingents, sending one to capture Harpers Ferry as a move to protect his line of communications with the Shenandoah Valley. The other moved westward through the South Mountain passes toward Hagerstown. Lee banked heavily on Little Mac's well-known slowness and caution. By the time the plodding Union commander closed in, the Army of Northern Virginia would be reunited once more.

But fate intervened. A Union soldier, lounging in a Frederick, Maryland, field recently occupied by the Rebels, spied a bundle of cigars wrapped in a sheet of paper. The paper turned out to be Lee's Special Orders No. 191, outlining the Maryland campaign and the division of the Rebel Army. If he moved fast, McClellan could realize every soldier's dream—to catch the enemy fragmented and destroy him in detail. The Union commander should have marched that night, but, being Little Mac, he waited until dawn. By then General Lee, who had learned that the Federals knew his plans, had rushed every spare soldier to guard the South Mountain passes.

McClellan was moving fast now, but the vastly outnumbered Confederates fought desperately and slowed him down. But when the bluecoats broke through and descended on the dusty Maryland town of Sharpsburg on Antietam Creek, Lee had less than 20,000 men to repel over four times that number (McClellan believed Lee's army numbered over 100,000 men!) The Confederates should have been engaged and crushed at once on September 16, before most of the Harpers Ferry detachments could come up, but Little Mac had to position his troops and attend, in a rather leisurely fashion, to every last detail before giving battle to the enemy drawn up along Antietam Creek. By September 17, when the Union Army attacked, all but one of the Confederate divisions

The Battle of Antietam, September 1862. (Library of Congress)

sent to Harpers Ferry had arrived by forced marches, and that one was rushing toward the battlefield.

The Confederates found themselves precariously situated at Antietam. Lee's outnumbered army stretched from its right near a bridge over the Creek, across low hills, then woods and farmland, to its left in some woods near a white Dunker church and a large cornfield north of Sharpsburg near the Hagerstown Road. The Confederates stood with their backs to the Potomac River. Escape might be impossible in the event of a rout. Even when Ambrose Powell Hill's absent division came swinging through great clouds of dust into the storm of battle late in the day, the Army of Northern Virginia was outnumbered two to one. But Lee's boys fought like demons all day.

When "Fighting Joe" Hooker led his army corps in a flanking movement designed to crush the Rebel left and roll up the whole enemy line, hard-pressed Confederates struck back hard and created a kind of "cornfield from Hell" with hands and limbs flying through the air amid artillery blasts, corn scythed down to ground level and blue and gray bodies piled everywhere. Two more big Union corps were wrecked here. In the Confederate center, Rebel defenders of a sunken road fought so furiously that when superior numbers finally dislodged them, the road became "Bloody Lane" because of the corpses strewn from end to end. And on the Union left, after stolid, unimaginative Maj. Gen. Ambrose Burnside had pushed masses of troops across Antietam Creek after maddening delays, Maj. Gen. A.P. Hill's timely arrival late in the day converted a Confederate rout into a stalemate.

The battle of Antietam abounds in colorful incidents: a Union attack on the Rebel left stopped cold by Texas troops furious because the bluecoats had interrupted their first solid meal in days; a Pennsylvania color-bearer losing a foot and striking blindly at a comrade trying to relieve him of the flag; men laughing wildly in the frenzy of battle in the cornfield. Confederate corps commander Lt. Gen. James Longstreet, a burly, bearded man limping about in carpet slippers, using an unlighted cigar like a field-marshal's baton to give directions, helping to aim an artillery piece in the threatened Rebel center; the 132nd Pennsylvania

Regiment fighting bees as well as Rebs after they blundered into a farmer's beehives; the boys of the 5th New Hampshire smearing gunpowder on their faces like Indians and charging down on the Sunken Road with a whoop and a holler. One New York soldier in the thick of the battle experienced an eerie phenomenon. "The mental strain was so great that I saw at that moment the singular effect mentioned, I think, in the life of Goethe on a similar occasion—the whole landscape for an instant turned slightly red."[16]

Where was Lt. Frank W. Dickerson, 5th U.S. Cavalry, during the bloodiest day of the Civil War? Frank's regiment comprised part of Brig. Gen. Alfred Pleasonton's Cavalry Division, which had been stationed at the Union center near Middle Bridge between Fitz-John Porter's Corps and that of Burnside. Pleasonton's horse artillery duelled with Rebel gunners across the Creek before the Division crossed to the west bank to support Federal artillery. General Pleasonton, queried by his commanding-general "Can you do any good by a cavalry charge?" wisely chose not to hurl his horsemen into the Confederate artillery and infantry meatgrinder.[17] And so "the entire Federal cavalry division, except for a few details tracking down infantry stragglers, idled away the hours in the valley west of the creek, taking cover from the shells shrieking overhead." To Lt. Charles Francis Adams, Jr. of the 1st Massachusetts Cavalry, the bombardment came to have a soporific effect: "I was very tired, the noise was deadening; gradually it had on me a lulling effect— and so I dropped quietly asleep,— asleep in the height of the battle and between the contending armies! Such is my recollection of that veritable charnel-house Antietam."[18] Curiously, cavalry-expert McClellan failed to utilize his horsemen to guard his army's flanks, a classic cavalry duty.[19] One doubts Lieutenant Dickerson slept under fire. Certainly a fragmentary letter, undated, reveals how this ghastly battle had seared his consciousness:

> *We gained a great victory over the rebels on the 17th and in fact have beaten them every time they have made a stand.—They succeeded however in getting across the river and escaping us. I will not attempt to describe the horrible*

Confederate dead near the Cornfield (Antietam). (Photo by Alexander Gardner, Library of Congress)

scenes I have witnessed—I have been over the battle field twice. I hope I shall never have to go over it again.—Though the rebels had 24 hours given to them to bury their dead yet the barbarous unhuman wretches left hundreds of their dead on the field and used the time in effecting their escape. Will a Divine Providence ever permit such villains to succeed in their attempts to break up this Union? The slaughter was terrible on their side. Our troops have been engaged in burying their dead ever since the battle. Their killed in some places laid in heaps and mud.—My paper is exhausted.
Love to all at home.

> *From your aff son*
> *I am well—*
> *Frank*

Samuel Fiske of the 14th Connecticut agreed as to the horrors of Antietam. He described blackened dead men swelling in the broiling sun.

There are hundreds of horses, too, all mangled and putrifying, scattered everywhere! Then there are the broken gun-carriages, the wagons, and thousands of muskets, and all sorts of equipment, and clothing all torn and bloody, and cartridge and cannon-shot, and pieces of shell, the trees torn with shot and scarred with bullets, the farm houses and barns knocked to pieces and burned down, the crops trampled and wasted, the whole country forlorn and desolate.

Another soldier wrote, "We were glad to march over the field at night for we could not see the horrible sights so well. Oh what a smell, some of the men vomit as they went along."

An almost palpable stench permeated the battlefield, a local farmhand recalling, "We couldn't eat a good meal, and we had to shut the house up just as tight as we could of a night to keep out that odor."[20]

Casualties numbered 12,410 for the Union and 13,724 for the Confederacy, making that the bloodiest single day of the Civil War, with twice as many American deaths in one day as fell during the War of 1812, the Mexican War and the Spanish-American War combined.[21] Incredibly, McClellan, fearing his own destruction, had held no less than 24,000 men in reserve. And although over 12,000 fresh troops arrived the morning of September 18, he refused to renew the battle, despite his 36,000 unblooded soldiers. That night, the Confederates recrossed the Potomac into Virginia.

The Army of the Potomac's cavalry rode after the retreating Rebels, only to be stopped by Confederate artillery. Next day, Little Mac sent two divisions "in mild pursuit" of Lee's army, now safely across the Potomac.[22] The great conflagration of Antietam had nearly sputtered out, but little flareups occurred into mid-November, and Frank participated in several of these skirmishes: Sheppardstown Ford (Sept. 19), Halltown (Sept. 26 & 29), Upperville (Nov. 2), Markham Station (Nov. 3), and Amisville (Nov. 11), all in Virginia. At Markham Station, sabre in hand, Frank led a charge against Confederate cavalry only to have his horse shot out from under him.[23]

General McClellan had promised an early resumption of the campaign against Richmond, but he moved with all the speed of a tired glacier! Even Lincoln's well-known patience had its limits. The Army of the Potomac needed a fighter at its head. And so on November 7, 1862, a staff general from Washington arrived at Little Mac's headquarters with orders relieving him of command of the army and replacing him with Maj. Gen. Ambrose Burnside. Outside McCLellan's quarters, a snowstorm raged as the transfer of command took place harmoniously. And then George B. McClellan rode out of the Civil War, never again to hold a field command.

Burnside, a big, burly, good-natured, 38-year-old known to his friends as "Burn," sported an intricate set of whiskers, puffing out on both cheeks and swooping across his upper lip, that gave rise to the word "side-burns." Life had had its disappointments: the loss of all the young lieutenant's money to an Ohio river-boat sharper as he traveled to the Mexican War; virtual bankruptcy in the 1850's when he failed to sell a breech-loading rifle of his invention to the U.S. government; even his Kentucky bride-to-be

29

President Lincoln visits with Maj. Gen. George B. McClellan at Antietam. The General was Frank Dickerson's first army commander. (Photo by Arthur Gardner, Library of Congress)

turning him down brusquely at the altar.[24] But his Civil War career had been, on balance, commendable until now. Burnside himself protested his unfitness for Army command. He was honest and brave but lacked the brains, military gifts and character to command a big force like the Army of the Potomac. But he would do his best. He hustled his troops to the lovely eighteenth-century city of Fredericksburg on the banks of the Rappahannock River, planning to cross there for a powerful thrust at Richmond. The element of surprise was crucial to the General's plan. But military red tape held up his pontoons. By the time they arrived, so had Robert E. Lee, strongly fortifying Marye's Heights back of the town. Rebel sharpshooters picking off Union engineers building the pontoon bridges were scarcely fazed by Burnside's massive and destructive artillery bombardment of the historic city. Finally, Federal infantry crossed in boats and cleared Fredericksburg, allowing the bridges to be completed.

Burnside, unimaginative and woefully stubborn, intended to press forward with his original plan, which Lee's arrival on the scene had rendered untenable. While the Union left struck hard at Stonewall Jackson's men behind a railroad cut on the enemy right, the Union right would storm General Longstreet's corp of the Army of Northern Virginia on Marye's Heights. Some 114,000 Federal troops fought in the battle against some 72,500 Confederates. Lieutenant Dickerson and his fellow cavalrymen, stationed near the Union artillery on the north bank of the Rappahannock, were spectators of the titanic struggle, reduced to despatch riding and orderly duty.[25] To them so far from the smoke, flame, blood, and smells of battle it must have seemed like picture-book war. The reality was sadly different. The Federals punished Jackson severely before he forced them back. But the fighting at Marye's Heights was totally one-sided, bloody beyond belief and almost beyond endurance for the brave Yankees. "Oh great God! See how our men, our poor fellows are falling!", a Union division commander cried[26] as well-positioned Rebel artillery swept the Union assault columns with shot, shell, and canister[27] from the heights. Massed Confederate infantry, ragged and wolfish, taunted

31

The Battle of Fredericksburg, December 13, 1862. Maine especially grieved over 50 percent casualties in the 4th Maine Regiment during this bloody battle. (Library of Congress)

Confederate soldiers massed in the Sunken Road behind the stone wall at Marye's Heights. (Library of Congress/Mathew Brady Collection)

the attackers to bring their fresh blue uniforms and knapsacks within plundering range as they made their impregnable position behind a stone wall into a fiery furnace. Attack after Union attack, with tossing flags, officers' swords gleaming, and men hunching forward as though lead balls were raindrops, swept up toward Marye's Heights. Some came within 25 yards of the stone wall, but not a single man reached it. General Longstreet had assured the worried Lee, "General, if you put every man on the other side of the Potomac in that field to approach me over the same line, and give me plenty of ammunition, I will kill them all before they reach my line."[28] Only night and senior general officer protests to Burnside stopped the slaughter. An officer of the Union Irish brigade shuddered at the scene as he described the horrors of the battlefield on that frigid winter night:

> A cold, bitter bleak December night closed upon that field of blood and carnage. Thousands lay upon that hillside, and in the valleys whose cold limbs were stiffened, for they had no blankets, they had flung them away going into the fight. Masses of dead and dying were huddled together; some convulsed in the last throes of death; others gasping for water—delirious, writhing in agony, and stiffened with the cold frost. The living tried to shelter themselves behind the bodies of the dead. Cries, moans, groans, shrieks of agony rang over the sad battlefield. There was no one to tend them; no one to bring them a drop of cold water to moisten their swollen tongues; for that field was still swept by shot and shell, and in the hands of the enemy.[29]

Sheltering among three corpses that night, his head cushioned on one and that man's overcoat flap helping to warm him, Lt. Col. Joshua L. Chamberlain of the 20th Maine, erstwhile Bowdoin College professor, had the satisfaction of routing several Confederate scavengers who would bolt when he spoke.[30]

The next morning the blue field had turned white. During the night, ragamuffin Confederates had stripped the corpses.

The Army of the Potomac withdrew the night of December 15. The Union had lost 12,653 men, the bulk of them at Marye's Heights. The Army of Northern Virginia suffered 5,309 casualties.

On Christmas Day, General Robert E. Lee wrote his wife:

But what a cruel thing is war. To separate & separate & destroy families & friends, & mar the purest joys & happiness God has granted us in this world. To fill our hearts with hatred instead of love for our neighbors, & to devastate the fair face of this beautiful world. I pray, that, on this day when peace & good-will are preached to all mankind, that better thoughts will fill the hearts of our enemies & turn them to peace.[31]

Surely General Lee captured the Christmas thoughts of Lieutenant Dickerson as he ended the most exciting and dangerous year of his young life.

CHAPTER III

1863:
Emancipation to Brandy Station

THE PRESIDENT OF THE United States rose from his giant bed early on a sunny, crisp New Year's Day, 1863. He had a busy day ahead. In the wake of the Battle of Antietam, Lincoln had issued the Preliminary Emancipation Proclamation declaring "forever free" those slaves held in bondage in States and parts of States under Confederate military control, if hostilities had not ceased by January 1, 1863.

The traditional New Year's reception at the White House began at 11 a.m. with an army of judges, diplomats, congressmen and officers in dress uniform, followed at noon by the "respectable" public. The President, his huge hands encased in white kid gloves, shook hundreds of hands until 2 p.m., when he climbed wearily to his second-floor study. Secretary of State William H. Seward had carried over from the State Department the printed parchment Emancipation Proclamation and spread it before the Chief Executive. Lincoln's right hand trembled as he inked his plain steel pen in its much-chewed wooden holder. "I have been shaking hands since nine [sic] o'clock this morning, and my right arm is almost paralyzed," the President observed to Seward. "If my name ever goes into history it will be for this act, and my whole soul is in it. If my hand trembles when I sign the proclamation, all who examine the document hereafter will say, 'He hesitated.'" So firmly and carefully he signed his full name "Abraham Lincoln" to perhaps the most momentous state paper ever approved by a President of the United States.[1]

With the stroke of a pen, the whole course of the Civil War

changed, from a conflict solely to preserve the Union to a struggle to guarantee that 4 million Southern slaves would be free in that restored United States. True, on January 1, 1863, not a single slave became effectively free, since the Proclamation applied only to areas under Confederate military control (Secretary of State William H. Seward commented that the Proclamation freed slaves where it couldn't reach them but left them in bondage where it could!). But it meant that Union armies became armies of liberation, freeing slaves wherever they went. And although the peculiar institution would not finally die until the Thirteenth Amendment to the U.S. Constitution killed it throughout the nation in 1865, an impressive beginning had been made.

Abolitionists reacted joyfully. "Thirty years ago," William Lloyd Garrison exulted, "it was midnight with the anti-slavery cause—now it is the bright noon of day with the sun in his meridian splendor."[2] Republicans, long advocating confinement of slavery and its ultimate extinction, heartily approved, too, many wondering what had taken Lincoln so long.

Democrats and conservatives generally denounced the Proclamation as a revolutionary initiative and called for "the Constitution as it is and the Union as it was."

Frank Dickerson's hometown reacted to the news of emancipation with similarly mixed feelings, Republicans like Judge Jonathan G. Dickerson supporting the President, Democrats generally condemning the measure. The *Belfast Republican Journal* spoke for the latter. Judge Dickerson's old paper loyally supported the war effort, doubtless relishing the following advertisement published on April 4, 1862:

War! War! War!
The People are Bound
To Preserve the Union!
They are also bound to
Save Their Money
And in order to do so, they ought to purchase
their goods of
A.J. Stevens & Co.

37

MICHELE LEACH

The J.Y. McClintock Block in Belfast, circa 1855. The building housed City Hall, as well as the Republican Journal, *which for a time was owned by Jonathan Dickerson. (Courtesy Waldo County Register of Deeds)*

Flour, Meals, Sugars of all kinds
Teas, Tobacco, Rice
Saleretus, Coffee, Spices, Syrups and Molasses
Pork, lard, butter, cheese, potatoes, fish etc.

And the *Republican Journal* noted with approval Judge Dickerson's patriotic report from the 1862 Washington Birthday celebration committee, prefaced by his own joy that "undaunted courage and persistent fighting of and by Northern men" had brought victory. (This was clearly a reference to Brig. Gen. Ulysses S. Grant's capture of Forts Henry and Donelson in

Tennessee earlier that February). "Events are demonstrating" the paper rejoiced, "that we have power enough to stand against treason in arms, and Europe in arms if need be. And thank Heaven, we are sending joy to union souls South."

But the *Republican Journal* denounced the Preliminary Emancipation Proclamation as "the most unwise measure ever undertaken by the ruler of a free people, the most stupendous blunder of the present unhappy contest, and as the legitimate progeny of the present dominant [Republican] party."

At least the Proclamation had

> cleared up all mists and defined the dividing line as sharply as need be, so a man is now an abolitionist or he is not, is either for maintaining the Constitution as the wisdom of the fathers who framed it . . . or for casting it aside and committing the country to the turmoils of revolution, anarchy, to butcheries, negro pauperism, and military despotism.[3]

Lt. Frank Dickerson's first 1863 letters take no position on the emancipation issue, indeed never mention the subject. A cavalry raid as a precursor to General Burnside's resumption of the offensive against Richmond engrosses him thoroughly.

> *Depot for Prisoners of War*
> *Assistant Quartermaster's Office*
> *Point Lookout, Md.*
> *January 7th, 1863*

Dear Father

I arrived here today with the cavalry command which has been stationed at Leonardtown and vicinity. We are on the eve of making a raid over into Virginia. I expect we shall leave here for the opposite shore tomorrow or Saturday night, shall be transported over by steamers under convoy of the Gunboats. I expect we shall land in Westmoreland Co. and run the gauntlet of the lower country between the Potomac and Rappahannock, destroying everything as we go, and subsisting on the country — that is if we have good luck and the opposition is not too heavy for us. We shall take over 150 regular cavalry, which will be under command of Lieut Mix of the 2nd U.S. Cavalry, and I shall be next in command. The Gunboats will also go up and hover round the Rappahannock, to protect us on that side. I suppose some infantry will accompany us and perhaps a section of artillery. I am well, received a letter from you the other day. My love to all at home and Mother and LuLu and accept much yourself from your most affectionate son.

F.W. Dickerson

Hon. J.G. Dickerson
Belfast, Maine

◆

Depot for Prisoners of War
Assistant Quartermaster's Office
Point Lookout, Md.
Jany 11, 1863

Dear Father

I wrote you the other day in regard to our contemplated raid over to Virginia, which has not yet come off, but probably will very soon. I suppose we shall leave tomorrow morning by 4 o'clock, land at a place called Kinsale up the Yeocomico River, thence to Warsaw Court House, traversing through the county to Lancaster Court House, through that county across to the Rappahannock where we expect to re-embark for this point again. I expect you will hear from us either for better or worse soon.

Aff'ny your son
Frank

Hon. J.G. Dickerson
Belfast, Maine

H.d Qur's Cav'y Det.
Point Lookout M'd
January 16th, 1863

Dear Father

We returned from our raid last evening having been three days in Va. once more.

We raided through Richmond, Northumberland and Lancaster Countys [sic], captured a large lot of horses, mules, cattle, sheep etc. (besides destroying an extensive tannery) a large quantity of pork intended for the rebel army. The raid was successful, only losing one man. The country we travelled over was very poor indeed, scarcely enough to subsist the inhabitants. Will send you some more particulars at another time.

In haste
Affectionately your son
F. W. Dickerson
U.S.A.

Hon. J. G. Dickerson
Belfast, Maine

General Burnside's performance at Fredericksburg had shaken the confidence of nearly all of his subordinate generals. Frank expresses alarm in his next letter about a resumption of the move against Richmond "by way of Fredericksburg," but he has little time to ponder grand strategy: the 21-year-old lieutenant finds himself temporarily in command of his regiment!

Camp 5th U.S. Cavalry
Near Potomac Creek
Station Jan. 17 '63 (1863)

Dear Father

I have just returned from a 3 days tour of picket duty. I had with me 75 men and two officers. — An immediate move is to be made by the Army of the Potomac.

*I understand that the whole army is under marching
orders. We have orders to be in readiness to move
tomorrow at 1 o'clock p.m. The Potomac trains have
moved up the river several miles above Fredericksburg. —
Should the army attempt to cross the river again and
move on to Richmond by the way of Fredericksburg, I
tremble for the result. I have no confidence in the move.
All our officers feel the same as I do about it, that the
army never can make a successful attack with the rebel
army in the position it now is. — I fear that if we do
make another attack on the rebel lines while they are in
their present position, that we shall meet with a stunning
overwhelming defeat, one from which we cannot
recoil and be driven, totally routed, back into the
Rappahannock. — God grant that it may not be as I
predict. But perhaps I may be mistaken in the movement
which is soon to be made, it may be (for aught I really
know) a retrograde movement. — This army, in my
opinion, must change its base — cannot be successful
from its present one. The army has confidence that
it can. —
Strange as it may seem to you, I am at present in
charge of the reg't. All the officers that are my seniors in
rank that have been with the reg't for some time past are
away on short leaves of absence. — Three of them should
have been back tonight. If we move tomorrow at the same
time designated, they cannot get here in season to move
with us, and I shall have to lead the reg't. It is a fearful
responsibility (for so young an officer and for one who
has had so little experience) and it rests heavily on my
shoulders, I almost shrink from it when I think of it, but
have made up my mind to assume it, to look boldly in the
face of all the difficulties which surround me in my
present position, and if I am called into action while in
command, trusting in God for help and protection, I
shall do my duty to the best of my ability. — It is the
result of the accident that I happen to be in commander,*

5 officers all my senior in rank, age, and experience, have left the reg't within as many days to go on short leaves of absence. Three of them should be returned tonight, among whom is our Comd'g officer Capt. Harrison. — Capt. Owens and Capt. Drummond are also away. Our reg't now numbers, I think, "present for duty," between 6 and 7 hundred men, we, having received two days ago, 225 recruits fully armed and equipped. — I feel that I am not competent to take command of so many men, but I shall have some sterling officers with me (old soldiers) (who will all lend a willing hand) and I hope for the best. —

I wrote Mother a few days since. My love to all at home and accept much yourself — From your most
Affectionate son
Frank

Most soldiers of whatever rank could scarcely believe that their commanding general would launch a full-scale campaign against the Army of Northern Virginia so perilously close to Virginia's rain and snow season. But on the balmy morning of January 20, the Army of the Potomac began leaving its Falmouth base, stepping smartly out on dry roads, heading for the Rappahannock River. A pessimistic Lieutenant Dickerson picks up the story:

Camp 5th U.S. Cav'y
Near Potomac Station
Jan'y 22nd 1863
Dear Father,
The army commenced to move on the morning of the 20th. All the infantry broke up their camps and marched up the river toward the fords where they expected to cross the Rappahannock. It commenced to rain on the evening of the 20th and rained and blew furiously all night, without intermission, and although it does not rain

today the weather has not cleared up yet. We have not left our camp yet, though we have had everything packed up (except our tents) for two days, and have been ready to move at 30 minutes notice. It was Burnside's intention to have commenced crossing at 5 o'clock on the morning of the 21st, but as yet none of our troops have crossed, but the elements (over which we have no control) prevented, and the army is encamped near the fords. The river has risen very much and the current runs so rapidly that it will be impossible to lay pontoon trains for several days even if we should have fair weather again. The general impression is that the movement will prove a failure, and that the whole army will move back and reoccupy the same ground that they did before the movement. The suffering of the troops during this severe storm must have been very great, as they have been exposed to the wet and cold, not even having the protection of tents which were all left with the wagon trains in the rear. We all considered that we were extremely fortunate in not having to leave our comfortable quarters during the storm. The camp of our brigade is situated along the line of the railroad in rear of the main body of the army and separated from them by Potomac Creek, which we have to cross whenever we go out on picket or go to the front. It is quite a wide creek, but the water has been so low since we came here that it could be easily crossed by Cav'y artillery and infantry. I crossed it on the afternoon of the 20th, it was not more than 3 feet deep in the center. Then we are obliged to swim our horses to get them across. Gen'l Hooker sent down an order yesterday for our brigade to come up and join the rest of the army, and Gen'l Averell sent back word that it was impossible for him to get his artillery across, and Gen'l Burnside sent back word for him to remain where he was until he received an order from him. The roads are in a terrible condition, our camp is a complete mud hole, and our poor horses have had to stand in it half way up to their knees, and have been exposed to all the rain and cold as we have no stables built for them. The men have nothing but shelter tents which are scarcely any protection from the rain. I have reasons to be thankful that I have a good comfortable tent, with a stove in it, a good bed, and plenty of warm blankets. While in camp we manage to keep quite comfortable, but when on picket, or out on scout, or reconnoitering, we encounter many hardships.

    I think the army will undoubtedly move back again to their old camps and movement across the Rappahannock [will be] given up for the present at least. They must do one thing or the other, cross or move back, for [if] it (the wet weather) continues, and we have every reason to believe it will, the roads will be in such a condition that it will be impossible to transport supplies to the army in wagons so great a distance from the R. Road. — No signs of the enemy have as yet been seen (from the ford where the army was to cross) on the opposite side of the river, though we have information that they know of our intended movement. I have no doubt but what there is plenty of them only a few miles from the banks of the river and, in the entrenchments too, for they have had time to fortify themselves quite well since the move was first talked of. —I wrote you only a few days ago and sent you a check for $150. I hope you will receive it safely. Capt Drummond is in command of the reg't now. Several of our officers who have been away from the reg't a long time on mustering, recruiting, and inspecting service, have been ordered back to the reg't and we are expecting them back every day. My love to all at home. Mother and Lulu. Yours affect.

Frank

Events bore out Frank's worst fears. Rain which had begun to fall lightly at first, soon came down in sheets and turned those dry sand roads into rivers of thick, gooey mud, seemingly

45

bottomless. "The whole country was an ocean of mud," one soldier noted. "The roads were rivers of deep mire, and the heavy rain had made the ground a vast mortar bed."[4] The cumbersome pontoon wagons, artillery pieces, indeed the whole army of the Potomac soon mired in Virginia's invincible "General Mud." Teams of horses were now doubled and tripled to pull the guns, to no avail. Hundreds of men hitched to ropes similarly failed, and cannon sunk to the muzzle had to be resurrected by shovel-wielding soldiers. Hundreds of exhausted mules and horses collapsed in the mud to be trampled to oblivion by other animals and long lines of infantry. One soldier who still retained a sense of humor wrote:

> Now I lay me down to sleep
> In mud that's many fathoms deep
> If I'm not here when you awake
> Just hunt me up with an oyster rake.[5]

This so-called "Mud March" required exhausting but satisfying service of Frank's regiment and other cavalry units—carrying rations and forage to men and animals stuck in the mud.

Januy. 23rd 1863

Dear Father

The movement of the army of the Potomac has, as I anticipated it would, proved a miserable failure. It is not the fault perhaps of the Gen'l Comd'g. The army is a dead lock. It is stuck in the mud near the ford where it was intended to cross. They cannot cross, neither can they move back, the roads are in such a condition that wagons cannot carry supplies to them, neither can the artillery return to the R.R. for the same reason. Last night our whole brigade was out carrying rations and forage to the troops. The wagons not being able to get to the army, the cavalry had to be ordered out to carry rations and forage to them on their horse's backs. I went out last night in command of our reg't and was engaged in carrying

supplies to the front from 5 o'clock p.m. till 5 o'clock
a.m., in the saddle all night long, and on strange roads,
dark as Egypt. — and up to the horses' knees in mud. —
We have a hard time of it I assure you. — The troops
were grateful to us for bringing them rations. — This
failure will demoralize the army to a fearful extent, it
must be the means of an immediate change of base. —
I trust the spirit of this army is not wholly crushed and
believe that with their favorite commander *[a reference to*
McClellan] once more at the head, and with a change of
base, the army may yet be saved. — It is reported that
Gen'l Lee sent word down to the ford yesterday that he
would send across a fatigue party to help up lay our
pontoons if we wished it, that he was prepared to give us
a welcome reception whenever we did get across.
P.S. The weather has been fine today. I rec'd yours with
*the postage stamps. [*Editorial Note: Perhaps there was
another page to this letter, or Frank forgot to use his usual
closing.*]*

After the ill-fated Mud March, General Burnside quarreled bitterly with his generals and urged that several be dismissed from
the service. "Either they go or I go," he told Lincoln in effect, and
the disillusioned President relieved Burnside of army command.
On January 26, he chose Maj. Gen. Joseph Hooker to replace him.

The new commanding general, a 48-year-old Massachusetts
native and a former division and corps commander in the Army
of the Potomac, had the blond hair, ruddy complexion (skin the
envy of any woman of the day, contemporaries gushed), and
bright blue eyes of a choirboy and the personal habits (so his
enemies alleged) of a practiced sinner. Hooker's detractors said
his pink cheeks came out of a whiskey bottle, and Charles Francis
Adams, Jr. huffed priggishly that under Hooker, "the headquarters of the Army of the Potomac was a place to which no self-
respecting man asked to go, and no decent woman could go.
It was a combination of bar-room and brothel."[6] And, perhaps

significantly, the term "hooker" as a synonym for prostitute is said to derive from his name. But few denied his gifts as a superb organizer of men and his uncommon bravery on the battlefield. His sobriquet "Fighting Joe" came from a newspaper misprint (the dash had been dropped from a battle report headed "Fighting—Joe Hooker"), but no one doubted his steely courage, symbolized by a wounded foot at Antietam.

"Now there is Joe Hooker," President Lincoln remarked. "He can fight, I think that is pretty well established. But whether he can 'keep tavern' for a large army is not so sure."[7] Fighting Joe could and did. Hitting the ground running, Hooker whipped his dejected army into shape, forcing his men to clean up their camps and themselves, breathing new life into the army's faltering food-supply and hospitalization systems, seeing to it that the troops received backpay, designing distinctive corps badges to symbolize unit loyalty and granting furloughs liberally.[8] Frank Dickerson refers to this last point as an integral part of the "administration new deal" in his letter of January 29.

Camp 5th U.S. Cav'y
Near Falmouth Va
Jan'y 29th, 1863

Dear Father

I haven't heard from you for some time, though I have written several letters lately in that direction—According to a recent order form the Head Qur's of the Army of the Potomac, leaves of absence to the commissioned officers, and furloughs to enlisted men, are now granted quite freely. All the officers that have been with the Reg't for some time past, have been off or are now off on short leaves. I put in an application the other day which was returned to me by the Comdg. officer, endorsed on the back that it couldn't be entertained just now as there were two applications in ahead of mine but he assured me tonight, as soon as one of the officers comes back that is now away, he would approve my leave — Lieut.

Sweetman, who is now away, will probably be back in less than ten days, when I shall renew my application for a leave, with a fair prospect of getting it. — In case I do, I think of making a short visit home — For the past two days we have had rain and snow in large quantities and there is now about 6 inches of snow on the ground, it has melted very fast today. Our horses have been exposed to all the rain and snow, and if it should now clear off cold — they will suffer a good deal — What do you think of the administration new deal? My love to all at home. Write soon.

Your aff. son
Frank

No reform of the new commanding general touched Frank as intimately as his reorganization of the Army of the Potomac's cavalry. Early in the war, Union Cavalrymen lacked the horsemanship of Confederate cavalrymen, the latter having been virtually born on horseback. And the Union conception of the cavalry's role in the war was as faulty as its equine skills. As Civil War historian Bruce Catton puts it:

> All too often the cavalry commands were split up and attached to separate infantry units, and there was a common tendency to employ them largely for routine picket and courier duty [also for escort duty, to cater to the vanity of generals!] . . . One result of this was that cavalry's standing was not high.[9]

The favorite infantry jibe was, indeed: Did you ever see a *dead* cavalryman?

The model for effective cavalry use, faithfully replicated by the North later in the war, was the Army of Northern Virginia's cavalry division, commanded by dashing Maj. Gen. Joseph Ewell Brown ("Jeb") Stuart, he of the red beard and plumed hat. Stuart's feared gray horsemen specialized in literally riding rings around the Army of the Potomac and keeping General Lee well informed as to enemy movements, for a vital role of the mounted arm was reconnaissance and scouting. Cavalry constituted the eyes of the army. It also could be, as Stuart demonstrated, a mailed fist, adept at smashing raids on enemy supply depots, railroads and towns. The key to effective cavalry use was unified command: stop dribbling horsemen away ineffectively as before; give them a fighting commander and send them, in massive numbers, on raids deep into the enemy heartland to smash enemy cavalry, destroy military targets, terrify civilians and bring back vital intelligence information.

Alas, Maj. Gen. George Stoneman, a stalwart but rather unimaginative and scarcely dashing regular army officer, was no Phillip H. Sheridan, the greatest of all Union cavalry commanders, but he might do. So Hooker hoped as he consolidated all Army of the Potomac cavalry into a single corps under Stoneman. Frank refers to this change in his next letter.

Camp 5th U.S. Cav'y
Near Potomac Station
February 12th/63

Dear Father,

I received yours of the 5th this morning and it was quite a surprise, not having received a letter from you for some time. — I have an application for a leave of absence already on file of the Adjts. Office and I believe it is first on the list, and will be forwarded as soon as one officer returns. — Capt. Harrison is expected tomorrow night, in which event my leave ought to go forward on the 14th, it ought then to be returned to me by the 16th or 17th, and if the application is successful, you can expect to see me at home about the 22nd of the month. I am going out on picket tomorrow morning and expect to be gone 3 days —

I expect to stop in Boston a couple of days and if I do I shall go out to G't Barrington to see Ellen.[10] I also will call on John Wayland — I shall stop at the American House in Boston, if I make any stop at all there.

50

I saw Horace Noyes the other day, he is looking finely, also saw Lewis Pendleton. Russell White was on to see me the other day. Major Cunningham told me that he expected to go home soon on short leave. I have no news to write of interest, except that the condition of the army is gradually improving under the vigorous efforts of Gen'l Hooker toward reorganization. Gen'l Stoneman is chief of all the Cavalry of the Army, the very best selection that could have been made in the whole army. We are glad to get him again and he is glad to come back to his old position. He reviewed us the other day, after which he called all our officers to the front, shook hands with us, and paid our reg't a high compliment.

My love to all at home, Mother and Lulu. Hoping I may be able to see you all soon, I am as ever

Your most affectionate son
Frank

Hon. J.G. Dickerson
Belfast, Maine

Taking formal command of his new cavalry corps, Stoneman parceled out the volunteer regiments between three divisions, while creating a "Reserve Brigade" under able cavalryman Brig. Gen. John Buford and assigning the five seriously under-strength regular army regiments to him.

"Special hosannas are due Hooker in any history of the Union cavalry for taking the long-overdue step of liberating it from the control of commanders of brigades, divisions, and corps of infantry and giving it a corps organization of its own," writes Union cavalry historian Stephen Z. Starr, who calls General Hooker's action "The emancipation of the cavalry . . ."[11]

Frank Dickerson expresses unfeigned delight at being emancipated from the volunteers.

Camp 5th U.S. Cavy.
Near Potomac Station Va.
Feb. 17th 1863

Dear Father

Since I wrote you last my prospects of obtaining a leave of absence unfortunately have not brightened, but on the contrary, have grown dim. I expected to receive my leave upon my return from picket yesterday evening, but neither Capt. Harrison nor Lieut. Thason have as yet, returned, and I can't go until they do. They have both exceeded their leaves some several days and have been reported as "absent without leave" — it is quite doubtful if I can get any leave at all, though General Stoneman told us he intended to give us all a chance. — Do not expect me home at present, at any rate not before the last of the month. I then shall be able to remain at home 3 or 4 days at the most, as I don't suppose I shall be able to get more than 15 days leave.

We are going to leave Gen'l Averell's brigade. All the regular cavalry are to be brigaded together and form the Cavy reserve of the army. Gen'l Stoneman will command all the Cavy and Gen'l Buford will command the regular Cavy brigade so we shall be under him. We are all glad enough, I assure you, of the change, specially so on account of getting away from the volunteers. The frequent association of our men with the volunteer cav'y, since we have been with this brigade, has done more towards demoralizing them, and destroying all principles of military rigor and discipline, than all defeats, disasters, or buffetings ever could do; while on the other hand, with the volunteers, the case is the reverse, the association of them with our men has taught them more than they could have learnt in a year's time if they have been alone, that is, they have taught them how to be soldiers in reality and some principles of discipline which they were entirely devoid of before. They have learnt all the duties of a soldier by observing our men perform

them in a soldier-like manner, also how to take care of
themselves, to prevent sickness, and how to live like a
soldier — With the volunteers, their carelessness,
uncleanliness, familiarity with the lack of respect to
officers, and superiors, and lack of discipline generally,
has had a tendency to impair somewhat the fine state of
discipline we possessed before we were associated with
them. —

Do not expect me at home, if at all, until towards the
end of the month. I shall come if I can possibly. —

My love to Mother and Lulu. — It has been snowing all
day long, some six inches snow on the ground, it is quite
warm. The travelling will now be worse then ever. I have
no army intelligence to write. Accept much love from
your most affectionate son

Frank

Hon. Jona Dickerson
Belfast

Frank's bare reference to his return from picket duty may have
masked something much more dramatic. His regimental historian
credits him with participating in a raid on the Orange and Alexandria Railroad at this time and, commanding 30 carefully-selected
men, wrecking the bridge at Rappahannock Station under enemy
fire![12]

A week after Frank's last letter, Confederate General Fitzhugh
Lee splashed across the Rappahannock at Kelly's Ford with 400
cavalrymen in a reconnaissance-in-force. He struck the Union
Cavalry hard near Hartwood Church driving in pickets, attacking
"[the] reserve and main body," and by his own claim, routing
them, chasing them to within five miles of the main Army of the
Potomac camp at Falmouth, inflicting significant casualties and
generally raising hell with the blue-coated horsemen.[13] A furious
Hooker reportedly exploded to one of his cavalry brigadiers:

> I know the South, and I know the North. In point of skill, of
> intelligence, and of pluck, the rebels will not compare with our

men, if they are equally well led. Our soldiers are a better quality of men. They are better fed, better clothed, better armed, and infinitely better mounted; for the rebels are fully half mounted on mules, and their animals get but two rations of forage per week, while ours get seven. Now, with such soldiers, and such a cause as we have behind them—the best cause since the world began—we *ought* to be invincible, and by God, sir, we *shall* be! You have got to stop these disgraceful cavalry 'surprises.' I'll have no more of them. I give you full power over your officers, to arrest, cashier, shoot—whatever you will— only you must stop these 'surprises.' And by God, sir, if you don't do it, I give you fair notice, I will relieve the whole of you and take command of the cavalry myself![14]

General William W. Averell, commander of the new 2nd Cavalry Division, was given the task and opportunity of punishing Fitz Lee, classmate at West Point and a good friend in peacetime. Frank's 5th U.S. joined the March 17 expedition, the regiment commanded by Capt. Marcus A. Reno. In the face of enemy fire, the 3,000 blue-coat cavalrymen forced their way across the river at Kelly's Ford (inexplicably Averell had sent nearly a third of his command to police fords north of Kelly's and keep an eye out for the Rebels). Frank's regiment formed part of Averell's right flank as the troopers advanced against the enemy. Lee had only 800 men but he struck at the Union left, where Col. Alfred Duffié's brigade countercharged and with flashing sabres routed the Confederate right flank. The Federals forced back the Rebel left, too, then aligned themselves properly and trotted forward through a forested area beyond which they were hit by Lee again, counterattacked and beat back both the Confederate general's left and right wings. But Averell's men were now within killing range of Lee's artillery, and the Union general, jumpy at rumors of Confederate infantry on the march to Lee's rescue, decided to withdraw, with not a man lost re-crossing the Rappahannock.[15] When Averell's old chum Fitz Lee had attacked the Union cavalry at Hartwood Church, he had left a message inviting a return visit and requesting a sack of coffee. The Union commander had shoved a bag of coffee in his saddlebag and left it on the battle-field with a note: "Dear Fitz. Here's your coffee. Here's your visit. How do you like it? Averell."[16]

Fitz could not have liked it much. Union troopers had more than held their own with the supposedly superior Rebel horse-men in a horse-back battle; in fact, a general with a true jugular instinct like Phil Sheridan could probably have finished Lee off. Lee's crows of victory were nonsense, and Frank and his fellow troopers could rightly feel proud of their achievement, especially since the 5th U.S. Cavalry, "At the second attempt of the enemy to rally . . . seized the opportunity and made a brilliant charge which forced them into a rapid retreat and won the commenda-tion of General Averell."[17]

Casualties at Kelly's Ford numbered 78 for the Federals and 133 for the Confederates. The saddest of the latter was the death of Maj. John Pelham, Jeb Stuart's almost unbelievably handsome, romantic and daring artilleryman who had distinguished himself under fire at Fredericksburg. The "gallant Pelham," as history knows him, had just returned from a courting expedition and joy-fully rode with Fitz Lee, a spectator since his guns were back at Fredericksburg. As he waved his sword, and rode into battle, a shell burst over his head and laid out the 23-year-old Alabamian, his dying body unmarred save for a deep gash at the back of his head where a shell fragment had bored two inches into his skull. Southern men and women (especially young women) mourned, his chief, Jeb Stuart, wept, and the war lost one more bit of gallan-try and romance.

By spring, 1863, Fighting Joe Hooker had transformed the Army of the Potomac from a dispirited force in Burnside's later days, into a magnificent fighting machine, full of esprit and opti-mism. Early in April, as Frank and his comrades passed in review before President Lincoln, who sat awkwardly on his horse with his elbows extending like a grasshopper's hind legs, the com-manding General's pride knew no bounds. He boasted of having the "finest army on the planet" and quoth, "May God have mercy on General Lee, for I will have none."[18]

His plan to encompass Lee's destruction depended heavily on

the new role he envisioned for his spanking new cavalry corps, commanded by General George Stoneman. The full corps, over 10,000 strong, would set out on April 18, quickly cross to the south bank of the Rappahannock, then knife into the Virginia heartland, smashing up railroad bridges, and rolling-stock, tearing down telegraph wires and uprooting railroad tracks, generally raising hell in Lee's rear with the object of cutting his communication and supply lines with Richmond and forcing his retreat. The Army of the Potomac would be on his trail, prepared to descend on the retreating gray army like a blue thunderbolt.[19]

As Lee retreated, Stoneman was to attack and harass Lee's army with all his might. "If you cannot cut off from . . . [Lee's] columns large slices . . . you will not fail to take small ones," General Hooker admonished.

> Let your watchword be fight, and let all your orders be fight, fight, bearing in mind that time is as valuable . . . as rebel carcasses. . . . It devolves upon you . . . to take the initiative in the forward movement of this grand army. . . . Bear in mind that celerity, audacity and resolution are everything in war, and especially is it the case with the command you have and the enterprise upon which you are to embark.[20]

But the "enterprise" bogged down on a soggy riverbank, the victim of torrential rain and a swollen river. The delay in the cavalry crossing forced Hooker to adopt, on April 22, a new campaign plan, one which ordered Stoneman to send elements of his main force fanning out to right and left to "inflict a vast deal of mischief, and at the same time bewilder the enemy as to the course and intention of the main body."[21]

The cavalry reached the Rappahannock's south bank on April 29. General Buford's Reserve Brigade, with Frank's 5th U.S. as a component, torched the Virginia Central Railroad bridge spanning the North Anna River, and destroyed considerable Rebel property (water tanks, supplies, etc.) at Trevilian Station. Other corps elements did even more damage, destroying bridges, ruining Confederate railroad property, capturing mules and horses, burning precious Rebel food supplies and freeing 300 Union prisoners.[22] Frank and his comrades returned to the Rappahannock on May 8, exhausted but exhilarated, by which time Joe Hooker had come a cropper in the murky woods around Chancellorsville.

The Union commander's magnificent army numbered 134,000 men. Lee had only 60,000 men to fend him off. Hooker's excellent plan, had it been carried out as formulated, would have crushed the Army of Northern Virginia between the jaws of a giant vise. Hooker, with the main body, would swing far to the west, then turn and move east through the Wilderness, an area of scrub oak and pine and tangled thicket, to Fredericksburg, still occupied by Lee. Meanwhile a smaller Union contingent would launch a diversionary attack across the Rappahannock at Fredericksburg to keep Lee busy and unaware of approaching disaster in his rear.

All went well at first; then General Lee acted with breathtaking boldness. Instead of retreating, as most generals in his fix would have done, he attacked on May 1. He divided his army, leaving 10,000 men at Fredericksburg to hold Federal General John Sedgewick and moving with the rest against Hooker's flanking force. When Lee struck his opponent in the Wilderness, the Union general, fearless and aggressive in subordinate command, found his nerve failing in army command. Instead of fighting on to the open ground beyond the Wilderness, Hooker surrendered the initiative, ordering his men to throw up fortifications near a big white-columned house owned by the Chancellor family. Here, at Chancellorsville, the confused and edgy Hooker awaited events. But he had not lost all his bravado, assuring his army that "the operations of the last three days have determined that our enemy must ingloriously fly, or come out from behind their defenses and give us battle on our ground, where certain destruction awaits him."[23]

On the night of May 1, Generals Lee and Stonewall Jackson conferred around a camp-fire, and Lee approved his corps commander's plan to launch a pile-driver attack on Hooker's exposed right flank, commanded by one-armed Maine native Maj. Gen. Oliver Otis Howard. Toward dusk on May 2, 1863, as Howard's troops peacefully prepared their evening meal, they were startled by a rush of deer, rabbits and turkeys through the camp. Then, shrieking the blood-curdling "rebel yell," Jackson's ragged gray-coats hit them like an avalanche. The Union right wavered, collapsed, and was driven back with heavy casualties, as night settled on the Wilderness. Black powder smoke choked the nightmarish place, rifles and artillery ignited leaves and undergrowth, and wounded men unable to escape the path of the fire committed suicide or roasted to death. During the night General Jackson and his staff, riding through the smokey forest, were mistaken for Union cavalry by trigger-happy Rebs, and the Confederacy's most brilliant field commander was severely wounded. Doctors amputated his left arm, but the intrepid Jackson succumbed to pneumonia, murmuring as he died, "Let us cross over the river, and rest under the shade of the trees."[24]

On May 3, the Confederates renewed their attack, and Fighting Joe Hooker, stunned when a cannon ball struck a Chancellor house pillar near which he stood, lost whatever fight was left in him. Despite the strong opposition of subordinate generals, the commanding General ordered a retreat across the Rappahannock, despite a large portion of his army having done no fighting whatever. General Sedgewick, who had fought his way across the river and taken Fredericksburg, was left to his own devices by the retreating Hooker and barely escaped destruction at Lee's hands.

Chancellorsville has been called the perfect battle. The teams of Lee and Jackson fought superbly, taking horrifying risks with confidence in their ability to out think and out fight a significantly superior enemy force. But Chancellorsville killed Jackson, and he could never be replaced. And although the Union had suffered some 17,000 casualties, the Confederacy had lost nearly 13,000, men most difficult to replace. For all its brilliance, the Battle of Chancellorsville was a mixed blessing for the South.

"My God! My God! What will the country say, What *will* the country say," an anguished President Lincoln moaned as he paced his office after the battle.[25] Little did Hooker know that in six weeks, he would cease to be commanding general of the Army of the Potomac.

Frank Dickerson makes no mystery of his feelings toward Fighting Joe Hooker in the wake of the Chancellorsville fiasco. His letter of May 23 provides some fascinating insights into the army's high command, suggesting that Frank had good sources of information available to him.

Camp 5th U.S. Cav'y
Near Brooks Station Va.
May 23rd 1863

Dear Father

I have to acknowledge the receipt of a long and welcome letter from you which came to hand last evening. — we left our camp at Bealton Station on the O. & A. R.R. on the 11th, but did not return to the army until the 17th after having been absent a month and 4 days. We are now camped near the R.R. about 2½ miles from Aquia Creek. Gen'l Stoneman, upon his return, finds that his rivals have been intriguing against him and have been trying to have him superseded in the command of the Cavy Corps. Averell, who has fizzled out by not doing the part of the work assigned him, and Pleasonton, who was left behind altogether in charge of the dismounted (2 sick men) and sick horses, on account of his incompetency, did their utmost to get Stoneman relieved while he was away; and, Gen'l Hooker, glad to find some one, if he could, to saddle the responsibility of his ignominious failure upon, had actually made out the order relieving him from his command for <u>incompetency</u> *and offering the command to Gen'l Meade, who refused to take it because he thought Gen'l Stoneman was the best Cavy Officer in the U.S.A. Gen'l Hooker in his jealousy and envy of Stoneman's great success, and chagrined and mortified at his own disgraceful failure, where he ought to have gained, and could have gained, a glorious victory and entirerly crushed out the rebellion, and fearing Stoneman would get the command of the* army from him, poisoned the mind of the President against him, and, to further show his displeasure, had Gen'ls Buford and Gregg who accompanied Stoneman, relieved for <u>incompetency</u>. But the outside pressure of the army and of the country was so great, upon learning of Stoneman's success, that Hooker was obliged to back down and countermand his orders against the Cav'y Corps. He is now doing all he can to perplex and bother Stoneman by cutting down and lessening his command. In regard to Gen'l Hooker's late campaign, I will say that I haven't seen an officer of the army yet who was in favor of recrossing the river. The only whipt man there was Gen'l Hooker, not one of the Corps Commanders except Sickles was in favor of the retrograde movement. At the Council of War, held previous to the retreat, Gen'l Reynolds rose and said that he was in favor of remaining there and fighting the rebels like h__l, then laid down and went to sleep. Gen'l Meade said, "Gen'l Hooker, if you recross that river now you are gone up forever." Sickles said that "his opinion as a soldier was that we ought to stop and fight them to the last, but if he gave his opinion as a man who had the good of his country the most at heart, he should say 'go back'." What he meant by that is more than I know. The rebels have not been so badly whipt during this war as they were at the time Gen'l. Hooker ordered the retreat, this they freely admit, this was one glorious opportunity lost. — There is no doubt but what Gen'l Hooker will be soon relieved, but, by when, it is hard to say. I am for Stoneman or Meade. The manner in which Gen'l Stoneman handled his cav'y during the recent raid has entirely convinced me of his ability to command the army as well as that he is one of the greatest Gen'ls of the war — It is now probable that nothing will be done until the conscripts are raised and sent into the field. Nearly 30,000 men have been discharged from this army since the recrossing the river on account of expiration of service.

We are having fine weather here now and very warm.
My love to Mother and Lulu and much for yourself from
Your aff son
Frank
Hon. J. G. Dickerson

On May 22 Hooker had replaced General Stoneman with 39-year-old Brig. Gen. Alfred Pleasonton as commander of the cavalry corps and ordered him on a reconnaissance march to find out why General Lee and the Army of Northern Virginia had moved west from Fredericksburg to the Culpeper vicinity. Another mission: attack and smash up Jeb Stuart's fabled cavalry division.

As the Army of Northern Virginia moved into position to launch a full-scale invasion of Pennsylvania, General Stuart found himself in command of a beefed-up division of nearly 10,000 men, and he decided to show off his troops in a June 5 grand review at Brandy Station near Culpeper Court House. The whole thing smacked of unreality in the midst of a gruesome war, but it was grand and glorious, a dazzling day with Stuart and his glittering staff riding along a road bright with flowers scattered by admiring women, thundering artillery, stirring music from three bands, thousands of Confederate horsemen in their best uniforms trotting past packed reviewing stands and, at climax, launching a sabre-swinging charge against that roaring artillery that thrilled the civilian spectators and caused some women to faint. An open-air ball climaxed the day (there had been another the night before), and although some critics commented sourly on Jeb Stuart's peacock pride and vanity, the whole affair stood in a class by itself as military spectacle. Three days later a less spectacular cavalry review took place before General Lee. General Fitzhugh Lee, the army commander's nephew, had invited General John B. Hood to attend the review with his "people," i.e. his staff. Hood interpreted the invitation literally and brought his whole infantry division— 10,000 men—to the Fleetwood Hill review site.[26] The review went well and General Robert E. Lee was duly impressed.

Jeb Stuart, his uniform and horse festooned with flowers, glowed with pride and anticipation as he contemplated future cavalry triumphs, and, symbolically, new plumes for his celebrated hat, in the forthcoming campaign.

In *Lee's Lieutenants*, Douglas Southall Freeman entitles the chapter on the Battle of Brandy Station[27] "Much Pomp Ends in Humiliation." And so it was. General Pleasonton, a dapper, bearded man given to straw hats and kid gloves, was known as a skilled military politician and self-publicizer, none too popular with his officers. But he had energy and ambition, and for the raid, he commanded the cavalry corps supplemented by two infantry brigades and six batteries of light artillery—some 11,000 men in all. On June 8, this formidable force moved from the Falmouth camps to the Rappahannock River fords. General John Buford, commanding the Reserve Brigade (including Lieutenant Dickerson's 5th U.S. Cavalry) plus a cavalry division, with Maine native Brig. Gen. Adelbert Ames's infantry brigade, accompanying, would cross at Beverly Ford, early on June 9, while six miles downstream at Kelly's Ford, the divisions of General David M. Gregg and Col. Alfred N. Duffié, with the second infantry brigade supporting and with Gregg in overall command, would elbow their way across the river. If all went well, the Union cavalry columns would proceed to catch Rebel cavalry in a coordinated three-pronged movement and whip the legendary Confederate leader.

At dawn on June 9, lead elements of General Buford's 3,000 man division splashed through the shallows of Beverly Ford and scrambled up the muddy bank to catch the Confederate pickets unprepared. While the reserve picket horses of both armies' cavalry were customarily saddled for instant action, this time the Rebels had neglected that sensible precaution. Buford's troopers barrelled through the startled graycoats like bulls through cobwebs, and would have captured Stuart's artillery parked near the ford had not 100 troopers of the 6th Virginia, some half-dressed and riding bareback, crashed into them and bought time to hustle the guns to safety. Rebel Brig. Gen. William E. Jones, an irascible, rough-hewn character nick-named "Grumble," arrived still

Brandy Station, June, 1863, the biggest, most spectacular cavalry battle of the entire Civil War. It was here that Frank Dickerson suffered a head wound; he was not to see battle again. (Culver Pictures)

pulling on his home-spun clothing, leading the 7th Virginia. The two Virginian regiments fought a heroic delaying action. Some additional Confederate cavalry and artillery arrived on the scene, and formed a stout defensive line behind a stone wall at St. James's Church between Beverly Ford and Fleetwood Hill, just beyond which lay Brandy Station.

Buford, faced with the prospect of charging the stone wall over a half-mile stretch of open field, didn't hesitate. The 6th U.S., with the 6th Pennsylvania supporting, drew sabres and moved on the enemy, first at a trot, then a gallop. Maj. James F. Hart of Stuart's horse artillery describes this spectacular action:

> The charge was made over a plateau fully eight hundred yards wide, and the objective point was the artillery at the Church. Never rode troopers more gallantly than did those steady Regulars, as under a fire of shell and shrapnel, and finally of canister, they dashed up to the very muzzles, then through and beyond our guns, passing between [Wade] Hampton's left and Jones's right. Here they were simultaneously attacked from both flanks and the survivors driven back.[28]

Buford had to pull back to some sheltering woods, but action continued on his front most of the day. Lt. Frank Dickerson "was conspicuous for dash and impetuosity at the battle of Beverly Ford, where the squadron he commanded received the first shock of the contest." As he lead a charge, a minié-ball[29] struck him on the head. It may have been a spent bullet or a glancing blow, but Frank was carried from the field, out of battle for good.[30]

General Stuart had slept under canvas on Fleetwood Hill on the night of June 8, only to be awakened by the rumble of gunfire at Beverly Ford. He sprang into action, Fearing a second Federal crossing at Kelly's Ford, he sent Brig. Gen. Beverly H. Robertson's brigade to guard the main road from Kelly's to Brandy Station. Two regiments were hustled off to beef up the rear of the Rebel defenses at St. James's Church, and the cavalry's wagon train creaked off toward safety at Culpeper. Stuart, after posting his aide Maj. H.B. McClellan (a kinsman of Little Mac) as a message relayer on Fleetwood Hill, galloped off to take charge of things at

St. James's Church. Here, the Union Reserve Brigade, increasingly threatened by Confederate reinforcements, realigned itself, placing increasing reliance on its infantry support element, commanded by Brig. Gen. Adelbert Ames.[31]

Meanwhile, a tardy Colonel Duffié had finally crossed the Rappahannock, his delay also holding up his chief, General Gregg, so that the Kelly's Ford force only arrived on the far side of the river at 8 a.m., four hours after General Buford began fighting. Gregg despatched Duffié's force to Stevensburg, there to cut off Stuart's retreat, while he himself set out with the rest of the command toward Fleetwood Hill. Confederate General Robertson, just turned 36, a balding man with soulful eyes, a thick black mustache and graying, scraggly beard, guarded the Kelly's Ford— Brandy Station road with his 1,500 man brigade. But Gregg led his troopers along an alternative route which added four miles to his journey but avoided the Rebel brigade. Robertson obeyed his orders to the letter and stood pat, showing no gumption or initiative even when he had reason to know the bluecoats were moving past his right flank. And so Gregg reached Fleetwood Hill unbloodied. This could have meant total Confederate defeat had Gregg barrelled onto the hill, brushing aside the startled handful of Rebels with their single cannon, and strongly fortifying this key position. As it was, the Union troopers twice captured the hill, but lost it twice to the Rebel cavalry rushed to the rescue by Stuart.

What ensued on the top and slopes of Fleetwood Hill was a wild free for-all of regiment against regiment, squadron against squadron, man against man, pistol against sabre, blade against blade, artillery sponge-staff against sabre, all fought in great and obscuring clouds of dust punctuated by roaring artillery and the screams of wounded and dying men and horses. As Stephen Z. Starr puts it, "[M]en rode in every direction, sabering or shooting down anything that crossed their path, and being sabred or shot themselves."[32]

One Union artillery shell ricocheted viciously, severing a Rebel colonel's foot at the ankle, passing through his horse's body, then ripping a hole in the body of a neighboring horse and emerging to sever the other rider's leg! A well-sharpened cavalry sabre, wielded by a burly trooper with his horse's momentum adding to the impact, could be a fearful weapon, and army troopers on both sides suffered sword wounds that bloody day. When the dust had cleared and the Confederates finally held Fleetwood Hill commandingly, the battlesite looked and smelled like a slaughterhouse.

General Gregg, driven south from Fleetwood Hill, joined forces with Colonel Duffié's column which he had ordered up from Stevensburg. Duffié had fought little and had played no role at all in the wild Fleetwood Hill melée. The French colonel's presence there might have made all the difference. As it was, Gregg and Duffié re-crossed the Rappahannock, leaving Stuart to face Buford from a powerful new fortified line running the length of Fleetwood Hill. Further fighting ensued before Pleasonton, spooked by rumors of Confederate infantry approaching (in fact a Rebel division did reach the battlefield but only after the fight at Fleetwood was effectively over), ordered him to cross the river.

Had Stuart's cavalry division been located at Culpeper Court House, as Pleasonton believed, instead of in the Brandy Station locality, the Union general would have met him with a unified command and might have defeated him decisively. Pleasonton failed to provide strong, aggressive, leadership of the Jeb Stuart variety and lacked that general's jugular instinct. And Stuart, while he fought superbly, had unquestionably been caught unawares. The Rebels could claim victory, driving their enemy from the field and across the Rappahannock and inflicting heavier casualties (866 killed, wounded and missing) than they suffered (51 killed, 250 wounded and 132 missing). But the real significance of this, the biggest, most spectacular cavalry combat of the entire Civil War, is what is showed about the Union cavalry. As Trooper J. N. Opie of the 6th Virginia summed it up, "In this battle, the Federal cavalry fought with great gallantry, and . . . they exhibited marked and wonderful improvement in skill, confidence and tenacity."[33] Well-mounted, well-trained, and with a kind of reckless courage, they had held their own against the Confederacy's best horsemen.

For the rest of his tragically short life, Frank Dickerson could take pride in his participation in the Battle of Brandy Station (or Beverly Ford, as it is called alternatively). He had played a part of conspicuous gallantry, but his untimely head wound and other ailments would cut short a combat career which might have carried him to high rank by 1865. Frank's war was now to take a very different turn.

CHAPTER IV

New Directions

SOON AFTER BEING WOUNDED at Brandy Station, Frank went on sick leave to Belfast. In contrast to the quiet of his hometown by the bay, the war roared on, reaching a tremendous crescendo during the first week of July. The Union cavalry which had nearly whipped Jeb Stuart at Brandy Station brought back information of his imminent movement into Maryland. The Confederate strategic plan soon became abundantly clear: the invasion of Pennsylvania.

The Army of the Potomac had a new commander. General Hooker had quarreled bitterly with Union General-in-Chief Henry W. Halleck over the command of the Harper's Ferry garrison. Hooker resigned suddenly, hoping to force his superior's surrender, but President Lincoln quickly accepted his resignation and replaced Fighting Joe with one of his severest critics, General George Gordon Meade. A quietly religious and highly competent soldier with a long, bearded face, Meade was a military martinet whose troops dubbed him "that damned goggle-eyed old snapping turtle."[1] Lincoln, noting that Meade was a native Pennsylvanian, used a barn-yard metaphor to speculate that the new commander, like a feisty rooster, would "fight well on his own dung-hill."[2] He did. The greatest battle ever fought on American soil spread out over three brutally hot July days (1-3) at Gettysburg, Pennsylvania. The two armies blundered together in the little market town partly because Jeb Stuart, off on a wide-ranging cavalry raid to redeem his near-defeat at Brandy Station, was in no position to provide General Lee with timely information on Army of the Potomac movements. The battle pitted nearly 65,000

Confederates against over 85,000 Union soldiers. After two days of bloody fighting, the Rebels had failed to outflank the massive blue army dug in on Cemetery Ridge. In a final, all-out effort on July 3, General Lee launched a 15,000-man assault column under the command of Maj. Gen. George Pickett aimed at the Union center. After an earth-shaking artillery duel unprecedented in American history, the Confederates marched forth from Seminary Ridge to cross the half-mile or more of open fields separating them from the enemy. Suddenly war had once again become pageant and spectacle. A Confederate battle line a mile from end to end, ranks two and three deep, moved majestically across the field. Georgia Brigadier Lewis Armistead led his men proudly, his hat on the tip of his sword as a talisman. Ironically, one of his dearest friends from prewar days, dashing Maj. Gen. Winfield Scott Hancock, commanded at the Union center.

Union long-range artillery ammunition had been mostly used up in the duel, so the Rebels came quite close to their objective before canister from the big guns, and infantry fire, began to tear into their parade-ground ranks. Union infantry caught both the Rebel left and right in murderous fire. Federal canister exploded into the gray ranks like giant shotgun shells, sending fragments of equipment and human flesh and bones flying through the air to the accompaniment of shrieks of agony. The whole battlefield smoked and blazed and echoed with a "vast mournful roar." Both gray-clad flanks had been punched in, but Pickett's center still had plenty of fight left. Now the Rebs opened fire, crowding in on the Union defenders with masses of men. Briefly they broke the Federal line, and fierce fighting with bayonet, clubbed muskets, and even fists boiled across the stone wall defended by the Union troops around the clump of trees behind. But now blue-coat reinforcements poured in and drove the Rebels back. General Armistead lay among the dead. He had led the 3,200 Confederates who had penetrated the Union line most deeply but would never see his friend Hancock again. General Meade, surveying the scene and realizing the victory won that day, removed his hat and murmured, "Thank God." General Lee rallied the survivors of Pickett's Charge, exclaiming sorrowfully, "It is all my fault."[3] Casualties in killed, wounded and missing overwhelm the mind: for the Union, 23,049, for the Confederacy 20,451, the latter virtually irreplaceable. From now on, the Army of Northern Virginia, which limped back into Virginia, could fight only a desperate, defensive war.

Bells all over the Union pealed with special joy and triumph on July 4, and the days following, celebrating not only "four score and seven years" of nationhood but also the great victory at Gettysburg and the surrender of the Mississippi River fortress city of Vicksburg to General Ulysses S. Grant. Flags flew and bells rang when news of Vicksburg reached Belfast on July 7. Frank Dickerson must have taken special satisfaction in the Army of the Potomac's triumph at Gettysburg, especially the prowess of the Union cavalry, which repulsed Jeb Stuart's gray-coats after a pitched battle featuring both furious combat on horseback and tenacious fighting dismounted. Doubtless he wished he could have been there. But recovery from his head wound was a slow process.

On July 16, 1863, Dr. Samuel B. Hunter of Machias, military surgeon of the 5th Maine District of Maine, headquartered in Belfast, wrote to certify that

> I have examined this officer, [Frank W. Dickerson] and find that he is suffering from gunshot wound of the head recd in Va 9th June 1863. And that in consequence thereof he is, in my opinion, unfit for duty. I further declare my belief that he will not be able to resume his duties in a less period than thirty days. The wound is doing well, but slight exertion gives headache and other symptoms which render it absolutely necessary that the patient be kept quiet.[4]

Dr. Hunter held office under the Federal Enrollment Act of March 3, 1863, necessary because recruiting in the States no longer provided sufficient troops for the Union armies. Gone were the days when young men fought to sign up, terrified of missing the war, which they assumed would be short and glorious. Now a board of enrollment consisting of a provost-marshal, a commissioner and a surgeon was mandated for each

MICHELE LEACH

The C.P. Carter & Co. shipyard on the Belfast waterfront, circa 1855. (Courtesy Waldo County Register of Deeds)

congressional district to implement the draft. Belfast was head-quarters for the 5th Maine District board.

The Civil War had engrossed the city's life and consciousness since Fort Sumter. More young men than required for initial regiments crowded into town and were somehow accommodated in April and May, 1861. Belfast companies joined the 4th Maine Regiment and marched off to war. First Manassas horrified Belfast's citizens, although they rejoiced that none of the city's young men had died at the bloody battle by Bull Run. This first Union defeat simply steeled Belfast's determination to see the thing through to ultimate victory. During the summer and fall of 1861, no less than nine recruiting offices flourished in the little city, with 1,000 recruits enlisted before the end of the year. That same fall, Belfasters celebrated the launching of the gunboat *Penobscot*, 158 feet long, 28 feet broad, 12 feet deep, and 550 tons of fighting ship bristling with a dozen 32-pounders (cannon capable of firing projectiles of that weight) and a pivot rifled gun. Meanwhile, the ladies of Belfast sewed furiously and sent countless articles of clothing to their boys in blue. A steady stream of items such as food parcels, sewing-kits and other knickknacks flowed from Belfast to the war-front.

Recruiting continued brisk in Belfast throughout 1862, but as 1863 began, national recruiting fell off as shock, disillusionment and general war weariness set in. (Belfast especially mourned 50% casualties in the 4th Maine Regiment at the Fredericksburg bloodbath in December, 1862.)[5]

On March 3, President Lincoln signed "An Act enrolling and calling out the National Forces, and for other purposes." E.B. Long summarizes its provisions.

> This, the first effective Federal draft, imposed liability on all male citizens between twenty and forty-five with the exception of the physically or mentally unfit, men with certain types of dependents, those convicted of a felony, and various high Federal and state officials. Draft quotas for each district would be set by the President on the basis of population and the numbers of men already in the service from each district. A drafted man could hire another as a substitute or purchase his way out for $300.[6]

Actually the draft stimulated volunteering, with men preferring to sign up voluntarily rather than being conscripted. Only 165,535 men, approximately 6% of the total Union enrollments, were drafted.

Belfast, in common with towns throughout Maine and the nation, worked hard to raise recruits rather than having to resort to the draft. Eventually a $300.00 bounty was authorized, with additional funds contributed by those liable to be drafted. Before 1863 ended, Belfast had filled its quota almost entirely with volunteers. In February, 1864 the little city avoided the draft entirely with the help of bounties, repeating this feat again in response to a July call for additional troops. In August, Judge Jonathan G. Dickerson joined eight other patriotic Belfast men, none liable to military service, in furnishing substitutes. A final Presidential call in December 1864 required 75 men from Belfast, the entire number volunteering by March, 1865. With the

MICHELE LEACH

The Waldo County Court House in Belfast, as it appeared around 1855, two years after it was built. (Courtesy Waldo County Register of Deeds)

exception of three men in 1863, patriotism stimulated by $300.00, city bounties had done the trick of allowing Belfast to avoid the embarrassment of having to draft its sons into military service.[7]

Certainly Lt. Frank Dickerson set his Belfast draft-eligible fellow citizens a sterling example of selfless duty and devotion to the Union cause. Although scarcely recovered from his head wound, he headed for the front during the second week of August, 1863. We find him writing home from Boston's Parker House on August 12.

Dear Father,
    I arrived here last night at eight o'clock, all safe and sound. — Have had a pleasant journey so far with the exception that it has been very warm. Saw Capt. and Major W'g in Portland also their ladies. Clara Emery

73

(late Sanborn) and Mr. Emery[8] *were at the U.S.*[9] *when
I got there and came on in the cars with us. They are
going up to New Hampshire. Mr. Emery was drafted the
same day he was married, heard of it coming in the cars.
I wasn't very well yesterday, but feel first rate today.
Ansel [White] and myself are stopping at the Parker
House, shall leave here tonight at eight o'clock for New
York — I had that deed matter attended to in Portland.
Mr. Rames was the magistrate I happened to call on, he
asked me if I was the "Judges son?" and inquired for you.
My love to Mother, Ellen, and Lulu and to Miss Allen.*
   Accept much love from your most affectionate son
                              Frank
*Hon. J.G. Dickerson
Belfast
P.S. Please write me at Washington. The following will
be my address.*
   *Lieut. F.W. Dickerson
   5th U.S. Cav'y
   Washington City*

Frank arrived in Washington to find that his brigade and regiment had reached the city the same day. He became company commander temporarily, as the 5th U.S. took up quarters at Camp Buford, Maryland.

                    *Camp 5th U.S. Cal'y
                    Camp Buford, Md
                    Aug 18th, 1863*
*Dear Father,
   I arrived in Washington last Friday, as well as I was
when I left home, except somewhat fatigued by the
journey. Our brigade with our reg't arrived in
W[ashington] same day. It was a mistake about their
being there before. Our brigade turned in all their old*

horses to the volunteer rgts., together with arms and equipments and have come over here to get remounted and new equipments. It is rumored that we are going on to New York to assist in enforcing the draft[10] but we don't give the report much credence. We are being supplied with horses as fast as possible.

I reported to Capt. Mason who is in command of our reg't this morning, and also took command of my company. I do not have to do any duty except camp duty — our regt is very much reduced at present in numbers. If the regt. moves away from here, and I am not fully able to do active duty, I shall not be obliged to go, but can receive treatment in Washington.

I had some photographs taken the other day and will send you some as soon as I receive them.[11] I am expecting to hear from you every day. My love to Mother, Ellen, and Lulu, and regards to Mrs. Allen and Miss Ella.

As ever your aff. son
Frank

Hon. J.G. Dickerson
Belfast
P.S. Ansel White went down to the army Sunday.

Frank

P.S. I am quite busy today looking after company matters and haven't time to write more.

Frank

We are camped about 4 miles from Washington near the Lunatic Asylum.

◆

5th U.S. Cavy
Camp Buford Md
August 19th, 1863

Dear Father,

I received a short note from you today enclosing a letter from Capt. Leib which I perceived had been opened and probably read. We are still in the same camp as

*when I wrote you the other day, and getting ready for
active service in the field, I suppose as fast as possible. I
don't think we shall go to New York, but back to the army
again as soon as we can get a new fit-out. I am looking
every day for orders to be sent me either from home or
from The Sec'y of War.*

*If any official orders comes to Belfast for me I wish you
would remail to me at Washington immediately, so that I
can avail myself of them.*

*Lieut Urban, who was wounded when I was, has been
ordered on duty as Ass't Mustering Officer.*

*I have no news at all to write except that I hear the
army is falling back from the Rappahannock. —*

*My love to Mother, Ellen, and Lulu and regards to Mrs.
and Miss Allen.*

*Couldn't I be ordered on duty at some other place, if
not in Maine! I think I am full as well if not better than
when I left home.*

> *Aff'y Your Son*
> *Frank*

Hon. J.G. Dickerson

The Army of the Potomac fought no major battles during the
remainder of 1863. But fighting boiled around the great Confederate rail center of Chattanooga, Tennessee, on the Tennessee
River. On September 19-20, General Braxton Bragg, commander
of the crack western Confederate Army of Tennessee, whipped
Union Maj. Gen. William S. Rosecrans' Army of the Cumberland
in the bloody, gruesome battle of Chickamauga, fought in the
murky woods along Chickamauga Creek south of Chattanooga.
The defeated Union troops streamed into the city's defenses,
besieged by Bragg's triumphant gray-coats.

Meanwhile, things remained relatively quiet on the Potomac.
Frank describes routine cavalry duties in his next letter.

H'd Qurs 5th Cavl
Camp Buford, Md.
September 24, 1863

Dear Father,

*I have received one or two letters from home of late
which I believe I have not yet answered. I wrote you last
at Alfred Me., about a week ago.*

*We are still in the same camp, refitting and drilling our
men and horses as fast as possible, it is impossible to tell
when we shall go to the front again, perhaps not this
winter though that is hardly possible, circumstances that
transpire in the Army of the Potomac will govern
probably all our movements. We are encamped about 5
miles from Washington on the Maryland shore near the
river, and though we have no picket duty to perform, we
have enough camp duties to attend to, two drills a day,
recitation of officers to the Comdg Officer, recitation of
new commissioned officers to their company commander,
besides all the roll calls to attend, as well as two stable
calls, and all duties relating to a strictly disciplined
camp.*

*I am glad you all enjoyed your visit to New Hampshire
so much and regret exceedingly my not being able to visit
my friends and relatives there with you. I am glad Ellen
has returned to G't. Barrington and think that her
improvement there during the past year would well
warrant such a step — I shall write her soon — I have
been very busily engaged during the past 3 weeks as Judge
Advocate of a General Court Martial which will account
for my not writing home any oftener. I had 103 sheets of
paper all written on in my court martial proceedings. We
have concluded it now and I expect to have more leisure
again. I have had no news to write. It seems from last
accounts that Gen'l Rosecrans has been badly whipt. I
hope that late accounts will somewhat relieve the defeat
— Maine, thank God, has once more done her duty nobly,
and has led off in sustaining the administration and the*

*war. May Pennsylvania and the western states follow
in her wake —[12] The defeat of Rosecrans is rather
unfortunate, especially at this time.*

*My health is now quite good, am able to do duty here
and don't think it worth while to make any further effort
to get away. In fact I am, I suppose, as comfortably off as
I would be most anywhere.*

*My love to Mother and Lulu. I wish you would send on
to me per Adams express at Washington 1 pair of dark
pilot pants which I left at home and my military white
vest. —*

Accept much from your most affectionate son.

       Frank

*Hon. J.G. Dickerson
Belfast, Me
P.S. Please address me as follows:
  Lieut. F. W. Dickerson
  5th U.S. Cavy
  Cav'y Depot Camp Buford, Md.
  Near Washington, D.C.*

An elegant reception for General Stoneman and wife enlivens
Camp routine.

       *Camp 5th Cavl.
       Camp Buford, Md.
       Oct 2nd, 1863*

Dear Father,

*I have not heard from home since my last writing but
will write a few lines voluntarily.*

*We still <u>hold</u> the <u>place</u>, and if the government will
consent I think we can <u>hold it all winter</u>.*

*Last Wednesday [we] gave Gen'l Stoneman and wife a
reception at our camp. We had the camp fixed up
elegantly with evergreens, cedars etc., so that it looked*

like a garden; I have never seen the camp look so well before — We had an excellent cold dinner, gotten up by a celebrated caterer in Washington, which we sat down to about 5 o'clock. Several of the officers had their wives present. Mrs. Capt. Mason, Mrs. Dr. Porter, Mrs. Sweetman, and Mrs. Paden.

Mrs. Mason and Mrs. Porter are boarding at a house about a mile from our camp.

On the whole the entertainment was one of the most pleasant I have ever witnessed and everything passed off with great eclat. The band enlivened the scene with their fine music and the General appeared to be very much pleased and his wife also.

I have no news to write, in fact I hear none "now adays."

It is impossible to say how long we shall remain here, liable to go most any time. Gen'l [Wesley] Merritt, commander of the Brigade, has gone on leave of 15 days.

I sent you 3 of my photographs, will have some more taken before long. I am quite well. Love to Mother and Lulu.

> *Your most aff son,*
> *Frank*

Hon. J.G. Dickerson
Belfast

On October 3, 1863, President Lincoln issued a Proclamation of Thanksgiving, noting that "The year that is drawing to its close has been filled with the blessings of fruitful fields and beautiful skies" and urging national thanksgiving "on the last Thursday of November next, as a day of Thanksgiving and Praise to our beneficent Father who dwelleth in the Heavens for these and other bounties."

> And I recommend to them [the people of the United States] that while offering up the ascriptions justly due to Him for such singular deliverances and blessings, they do also with humble

penitence for our national perverseness and disobedience, commend to His tender care all those who have become widows, orphans, mourners and sufferers in the lamentable civil strife in which we are unavoidably engaged, and fervently implore the interposition of the Almighty Hand to heal the wounds of the nation and to restore it as soon as may be consistent with the Divine purposes to the full enjoyment of peace, harmony, tranquillity and Union. [13]

"Amen," Frank Dickerson must have murmured as he took up his new post at Point Lookout, Maryland:

> *H'd Qur's Det. 5th Cavalry*
> *Point Lookout, Md.*
> *Oct. 16th 1863*
>
> *Dear Father,*
> *It has been a long time since I have heard from home. I left Camp Buford with two companies of my reg't on the evening of the 9th and arrived at this post on the 13th. There are two regts of infantry only here and the post is under the command of Gen'l Marston of W. Va. He is a very clever gentleman but I guess not much of a soldier. I took dinner with him the other day and he was only social. We have nothing to do at all, save to furnish guards once in a while for the rebel prisoners that are here. There are between 4 and 5 thousand prisoners here, also one of the largest hospitals in the U.S. [Original letter torn—several words missing] . . . has again gone into the field — I may remain here all winter.*
>
> > *Love to all at home —*
> > *Affy your son*
> > *F. W. Dickerson*
>
> *Hon. J. G. Dickerson*
> *Belfast, Me.*

P.S. Direct your next letter as follows
Lieut. F.W. Dickerson
Camd'd Det. 5th U.S. Cavy
Point Lookout, Md.

Even before Frank's change of post, the usual jabbing and skirmishing between the Army of the Potomac and the Army of Northern Virginia had turned into something more serious. Learning that Meade's army had been weakened by Hooker's taking two corps west to the Chattanooga campaign, Lee took the offensive on October 9, trying to turn Meade's right flank in a move against Washington itself. A hot fight broke out at Bristoe Station on October 14, with Confederate General A. P. Hill bloodily repulsed. On October 19, General Judson Kilpatrick, commanding the Army of the Potomac's 3rd Cavalry Division, ran afoul of Jeb Stuart and was routed at Buckland Mills. Lee's offensive failed, but Meade tried unsuccessfully to force the Army of Northern Virginia out of its Rapidan River position. (November 26-December 1). Then the Army of the Potomac went into winter quarters in the Culpeper vicinity.

Meanwhile, Frank describes his light duties at Point Lookout, where he commands the small cavalry detachment. He itches for service in the field and "my share of the glory."

Head Qurs Cavil Det
Point Lookout, Md.
October 24, 1863

Dear Father,
I haven't received a letter from home for a month and I can only account for it in this way, that all my letters have been sent to the regiment instead of at this place and have not been forwarded to me. I am still at this post in command of all the cavalry here amounting to about 110 men, half of which are from the 2nd U.S. Cav'y. and the rest from the 5th. I have no other officer with me,

*Lieuts. Mix and Denney having gone up the country some
30 or 40 miles with the other hundred men, to enforce the
draft and law and order, as well as to look after
smugglers, deserters, and blockade runners that are so
numerous in this intensely secret region.*

*My duties are comparatively nothing, and were it not
for drills, parades, and inspections which I have, I should
be very lonesome. It is getting to be rather monotonous
down here as it is, though we have everything we desire
to make ourselves comfortable. There are only two small
regiments of W/Va. Vol's [Volunteers] here that do the
Guard duty for some 6 thousand rebel prisoners of war,
they intend to keep 10,000 here during the winter. They
have no fort here to keep them in, the prisoners live in
tents and their camp is enclosed all round by a high
board wall. The cavalry are kept here, I suppose, for use
in case of revolt and escape of the prisoners to scour the
country and hunt them down. The Gen'l [Marston]
appears to think a great deal of this little command of
cavalry, and gives us all we ask for. I think he will keep
us here all winter if he can, but have my doubts about his
being able to do it, there will be so many opposed to it.
The Commanding Officer of our regt don't like much to
have his regiment divided, it is small enough already,
and Gen'l Buford wants all the regulars with him, so
Gen'l Marston will have a good deal of army influence to
contend with in order to keep us here. 200 cavalry makes
quite a gap in the regular brigade. I have had an
opportunity since I have been here to find out what a
fine thing it is to be one's own commanding officer. The
General hasn't interferred with me as yet in any way
whatsoever, letting me manage the cavalry as I please.
It is considered a fine thing to soldier in a country when
there is no armed enemy to resist and oppose you, and
when you can go where you please without being shot at,
but I am getting tired of it and expect to find myself soon
applying to go into the field again. I left Camp Buford on*

the 9th of the present month, and on the 12th, two days after I left, our brigade (with my regt. in it) left for the front and to cast its destinies with the Army of the Potomac once more. Though I haven't heard from them since they left, I know they must have had a very hard time of it, and done good work for the cause of the Union, and I shall lose my share of the glory they may achieve.

My love to Mother and Lulu. How did you like the photographs of myself that I sent you from Camp Buford also those I sent you of Genls Stoneman, Buford, Kilpatrick and Pleasonton while you were at Alfred, Me.? Did you ever receive them? You have never acknowledged the receipt of them in any letter.

Accept much love from your most aff son
Frank

Hon. J. G. Dickerson
Belfast, Me.
P.S. I wish you would send some Maine newspapers once in a while. Don't fail to direct next letter as follows:
Lieut. F. W. Dickerson
Comd't Det. Cav'y
Point Lookout, Md.

Frank finds himself supervising a Maryland local election to prevent disorder and interference with voting in this slave state which has a considerable disunionist element. He could be very tough indeed when confronted by disloyalty, as his arrest of the "old aristocrat" suggests, although he shows a bit of kindness in his advice to the trembling old man before turning him over to the "tender mercies of the Provost Marshall." And his assignment has its exciting moments, as he gallops off in pursuit of escaped prisoners. But it can be lonely, too.

Head Qur's Cav'l
Point Lookout, Md
Nov. 13th, 1863

Dear Father,

*I have received two letters from home within the past week, one of which was forwarded from the regiment. I am glad to hear that all are well at home. Ellen has also written me in answer to a letter of mine, and gives a glowing account of how nicely everything goes at Gt. Barrington this term. —I am still occupying the same position (*Chief *and* Commandant *of Cavalry at this post) as when I last wrote. Last week I was away with my command all the week, superintending the election. I had some of my men at each voting district in this county and the people agree in saying there never was a more peaceable or quiet election. I arrested one old aristocrat at the polls, for uttering treasonable sentiments, and that too before he had voted. He was very much frightened but I told him he must be more careful in the future and not allow officers of the army to overhear him. — I sent him down to Leonardtown about ten miles from where I was, and turned him over to the tender mercies of the Provost Marshall. Aside from this there were no other disturbances and this is the strongest secession county in the state. —*

The other night 5 rebel prisoners escaped from the prisoners camp. I went immediately after them with 10 men, shot two of them, and captured the whole 5 again. —There are now here between 11 and 12,000 rebel prisoners of war, which are guarded by a mere handful of men as it were, only two small regt's of infantry numbering perhaps to say the most 500 men in both regt's. —I think I am more comfortably situated now than I have been at any time before since I entered the army. —My camp is in the Pines on the Point (a narrow neck or tongue of land) with the Potomac river on one side of me and the broad Chesapeake Bay on the other, both in full view and not 800 yds. apart — My men have nice large Sibley tents with stoves, plenty to eat and not much (comparatively) to do, also plenty of forage for the horses.

It is sometimes a little lonesome here. I am the only regular officer on this Point, though I have met several fine gentlemen among volunteers here. Many officers have their wives and daughters here, and friends both ladies and gentlemen are constantly coming to visit them, — so much social intercourse makes it quite pleasant, I can hardly realize it is soldiering, it reminds me of what it must be in peacetimes. Your letter which I received the other day, first apprised me that they were raising a new cavalry regiment in Maine. I should have liked very much to have had the Lieut Colonel'cy of it, I wouldn't have taken anything else, but if it is as you say, of course there was no chance for me, if there should be any, please let me know at once. — My love to all at home. As ever your

Most affe' son
F. W. Dickerson
5th Cav'l U.S.A.

Hon. J. G. Dickerson
Belfast, Me.

In November, the nation focused its attention on Chattanooga. General Grant, the hero of Vicksburg, had arrived to take overall command of the effort to break Braxton Bragg's suffocating siege. The half starved Union defenders of the Tennessee city cheered the re-opening of the food-supply line—the so-called "cracker line"— under Grant's aegis. And in late November, in the battles of Lookout Mountain and Missionary Ridge, Union troops cracked the enemy's siege lines and drove Bragg's army into headlong retreat southward. Grant's star, already bright, shone with new luster.

On November 28, Frank tells his father of new orders.

Head Qur's Cavl De'pt
Point Lookout M'd
Nov 28th, 1863

Dear Father,
I have this day received a letter from you in which you state you haven't heard from me for a long time. I cannot account for it as I wrote you some ten days ago (or a fortnight). I received orders today to return with all the men belonging to the 5th Cav'ly of the Army of the Potomac, and I expect to leave on Monday next the 30th. I am very well and am well satisfied with the change. As I am [a-tired?] of staying here — My love to all at home. I have to thank you and mother for several papers. In great haste I am as ever your affectionate son.
Frank
P.S. I will write again after I return to the reg't.
F.W.D.

But the order to return with his 5th U.S. Cavalry troopers to rejoin the Army of the Potomac had been changed. He will be stationed at Leonardtown, Maryland, for some time to come. At least his social life improves dramatically and, on the whole, he is content. But he still longs to rejoin the main army.

Head Qur's Cav'y D'et.
Fenwicks Hotel
Leonardtown, Md.
Dec. 5th, 1863

Dear Father,
I wrote you a short note about a week since, in which I informed you that in a few days I should leave with my command for the Army of the Potomac, but since that writing the programme has slightly changed. The order, ordering me back to the regiment, has been temporarily revoked, and the only change made in my status, is that I

*have come up to take command at Point Lookout. I am
very snugly ensconced in the hotel at this place where I
have my H'd Q'trs. and my men are comfortably
quartered in the Court House and my horses stabled in
the stables of the hotel. On the whole I am quite well
satisfied with the changes, if they will only let me remain
here any length of time. Leonardtown is quite a little
place, the shire town of St. Mary's County, and the people
although all secesh [i.e. secessionist] are very hospitable
and polite to us.*

*Last evening I was invited out to partake of terrapin,
wild duck, and oyster[s] which was truly elegant. I have
invitations out to dine and tea every day. Politics is a
subject which we never discuss as everyone knows what
my sentiments are (my uniform showing if nothing else)
and I know theirs — I have 110 men under my command
at or near the vicinity of this town. I have squads out all
the time day and night scouting around looking after
blockade runners who infest this country. — and while
the command has been here they have made many
important captures.*[14] *— I have one other officer with
me Lieut Denney of my reg't and the Gen'l sent word
to me yesterday, that he would send me two infantry
Lieutenants to report to me for orders.*

*I have received several papers from home for which
accept my thanks — Please continue to send them. I
hardly think I will stay here all winter, yet if the Army of
the Potomac is going into winter quarters I should prefer
doing so and think I could do more good here than there
— If I should be stationed here permanently, I shall make
a visit home sometime during the winter, as I can get a
leave of absence any time almost in the "Dept" — I have
no news to communicate. Direct your next letter to me at
this place — Much love to Mother and Lulu — and accept
the same for yourself.*

As ever Your Most Affectionate Son
F. W. Dickerson
1st Lieut. 5th Cav'y
Coma'd Cavy Det.
Leonardtown, Md.

Frank finds himself dabbling in Unionist politics.

Head Qur's Cav'l De'p
Leonardtown, Md.
Dec 18th, 1863

Dear Father,
I have the pleasure to acknowledge the receipt of several newspapers from home lately but not any letters. —
I am situated the same as at my last writing, scarcely any change since then, and it looks as if I should remain here over Christmas and the holidays, during which time I anticipate a good deal of pleasure, as the people in this state make a great deal of Christmas, both white and black. A union party is being organized in this county under the auspices — protection — of the military authorities. We had a small meeting at Oakville the other day, and I have a caucus here next Tuesday, when it is expected every elective district in the county will be represented. The caucus will call a county convention of unconditional union men of the county to be held at this place, and delegates from several towns in the county we hope will be present. — We also hope to be able to get some unionist speaker from abroad. [Henry] Winter Davis of Maryland if possible — The senior men of this county are most all poor men though honest, and the union sentiment never has, till the present time, had much of an opportunity to develop itself. It is increasing however now — and as much as we can. — My health

*remains good. I have nothing new to write. My love to
Mother and Lulu and accept much yourself from your
most affectionate son.*

"Frank"

*Hon. J.G. Dickerson
Belfast*

In his last 1863 letter, Frank notes that his command now comprises an element of the 18th Corps, which falls within the District of Virginia and North Carolina, commanded by Maj. Gen. Benjamin F. Butler. Frank passes up an opportunity to dine with this bulky, cross-eyed (Lincoln quipped that Butler saw things differently than other men!) and highly controversial general.[15]

*H'd Qurs Cav'y Det.
Leonardtown, Md.
Dec. 29th, 1863*

Dear Father,

*I have the pleasure to acknowledge the receipt of a
letter and several papers from you lately. I still remain
situated as at last writing which is as agreeable as I could
wish. — I expect to go to Washington for a few days on
official business, connected with this command,
sometime this week. — We have very little excitement
here, nothing stirring at all hardly except what you could
observe in any country village. The routine of life here
remains much the same, and is rather monotonous same
thing [nearly?] every suceeding day, not much like life in
camp when on active service in the field.*

*I am indeed glad to hear so good on account of Maine;
hope she will succeed in filling her quota by volunteers.
The draft will come off in this state sometime in January,
when I shall have work enough hunting up the conscripts,
preventing their escape into Virginia, for if they find they
have to go into the army at all, they prefer going into the*

89

*Confederate army than ours. We are new in the 18th
Army Corp, comprising the department of Virginia,
North Carolina, the District of St. Mary's, and Charles
Co.[unty] with a portion of the Eastern shore of
Maryland. All under the command of Major Gen'l B.F.
Butler who has his quarters at Fortress Monroe Va. The
Gen'l was at Point Lookout the other day when I was
down there, with several of his staff. I was invited to dine
with him at Gen'l Marston's Head Qurs. by his Ass't
Adjutant Gen'l but thought there would be so many there
I wouldn't go, was sorry after that I didn't, as I missed
seeing the second hero of New Orleans.[16] Gen'l Butler was
at the Point arranging about the exchange of prisoners.
Gen'l Marston will still retain command of this District
but will be subject to Gen'l Butler's orders and will have
to report to him instead of reporting directly to the War
Dept as before. Gen'l Marston is much pleased with the
change. —*

    *I am sorry Mother and Lulu are unwell, hope they are
both better by this time. If I am here by the last of
January, I shall apply for a leave of absence of 15 days.*
    My love to Mother and Lulu.

> *As ever affectionately*
> *Your son*
> *Frank*

Hon. J.G. Dickerson
Belfast, Me.

CHAPTER V

1864:
"Winding the Whole Thing Up"

THE JADED DESK CLERK at Washington's sprawling Willard's Hotel had seen them all: portly cigar-puffing politicos, with gold watch chains draped across their overstuffed vests; oily lobbyists and officeseekers on their way to or from government Departments or the White House; military officers without number of every rank and in every stage of inebriation from the delights of Willard's celebrated bar. And so he scarcely noticed the self-effacing, brown-bearded officer with the young boy who arrived the afternoon of March 8, 1864. A wrinkled linen duster mostly covered the man's uniform, but the clerk may have noticed the parallel rows of brass buttons grouped in threes signifying a major general. The officer learned that only a very indifferent room remained, shrugged resignedly and signed the register "U.S. Grant and Son, Galena, Ill." The desk clerk gulped, almost saluted the Union's most celebrated soldier, changed the room assignment to the best in the house and even carried the luggage.[1]

Ulysses S. Grant had come to Washington to accept personally from the President of the United States a commission as lieutenant general, to that time, save for George Washington, the highest regular army rank given to any soldier in American history. Now he outranked everyone in uniform. His task: to plan grand strategy and formulate campaigns to end the Civil War. The battered and beleaguered Confederacy, incredibly still alive after three awful years of war, stood on the verge of being pounded to rubble by a master of the art of deconstruction.

For the first time, Lincoln had a general capable of seeing the war on all fronts as a whole, an integrated problem demanding a comprehensive solution. All Union field armies would close in on the weakened Confederacy. In the west General William T. Sherman would lead 100,000 men in three armies (the Army of the Tennessee, the Army of the Cumberland and the Army of the Ohio) against the 65,000-man Confederate Army of Tennessee, now led by General Joseph E. Johnston, vice Braxton Bragg, as it strove to shield Atlanta.

Another federal force would crush out Rebel opposition in the lovely Shenandoah Valley, then ravage that vital Confederate breadbasket until it could no longer feed the Confederacy. Lieutenant General Grant would personally direct the 110,000 Army of the Potomac, still nominally under Meade's command, as it barreled toward Richmond, defeating decisively the 62,000 troops of Lee's Army of Northern Virginia on the way. Grant fully understood that enemy armies, not geographical locations, must be the proper targets if the war was ever to be won. As he told Meade in April, "Lee's army will be your objective point. Wherever he does, there you will go also."[2] For his part, General Lee vowed to destroy Grant's army before it reached the James River, knowing that failure meant the slow strangulation and agonizing death of his army and nation.

But these cosmic events lay just over the horizon as Lieutenant Frank Dickerson began the penultimate full year of his life. Now back in Leonardtown, he describes a raid into Virginia, with a typical Northern reaction to the poverty-stricken rural South; and the decreasing chance that he will be able to come home for a visit.

Leonardtown, Md.
January 25th 1864
Dear Father,
I received a letter from you some days since, as well as several papers from mother, I am very thankful for them. I am again in Leonardtown and situated the same as I was previous to our raid into Virginia, which, by the

way, was quite a brilliant [one], considering the small force we had to operate with, only 100 cavalry. We were separated from the time we landed in Virginia until the day we reembarked for Maryland again. 30 of our cavalry was [sic] detached to accompany the infantry command, which was under Gen'l Marston, while we were on our own hook, three officers with our party, Lieut Mix 2d Cav'y Commd'd (he being senior to me) and Lieut Denney 5th cav'y with myself. — Though we did some pretty hard marching, and passed through sleepless nights, yet we enjoyed the trip very much as it was a relief to the monotony that pervades our life of this community. The reason of our not accomplishing more in the way of destroying stores, running off horses, mules, cattle, etc., was because there was not anything more in the country to destroy or bring off unless we left the inhabitants starving. It was the poorest country I ever was in, and it is a wonder to me how they manage to live. Certainly they must suffer greatly at times for even the necessaries of life, while luxuries are unheard of. I have sent you a copy of the Baltimore American which contains a brief and very correct account of the raid — I have about given up the idea of coming home this winter, think I will wait until summer. I sent you one of my photographs taken a day or two after my return from the raid. My love to Mother and Lulu. As ever your most affectionate son.

F.W. Dickerson—U.S.A.

Hon. J.G. Dickerson
Belfast

Leonardtown, Md.
February 7, 1864

Dear Father,

I received yours of the 7th this morning and am glad to hear that all are well at home. I fear I shall not be able to come home this winter, as Lieut. Denney who has been here with me has been ordered to Washington to attend as a witness before a military commission sitting there, which will detain him sometime and thus he has received a leave of absence after ten days which will commence after he gets through there; we cannot both go away at the same time, and it will be too late in the spring when he gets back, that I don't think it will be worthwhile to come North but will come in the summer when I can enjoy myself much better. I am sorry to hear of Aunt Lucy's illness, hope that it is not serious. Everything has again relapsed into its old quietness here. — We expect to be relieved from here soon and to go [to] the front again, we congratulate ourselves on having escaped so many hardships of a winter campaign in Virginia. — I should like to make a trip North during this month but fear it will be impossible, so don't expect me. Thanks for papers which I receive from you and mother quite regularly

With much love for all at home. I am as ever your most affectionate son

"Frank"

Hon. J.G. Dickerson
Belfast, Me.

P.S. Please direct to me at Leonardtown Md. instead of Point Lookout.

In his long February 14 letter, Frank contrasts his detached duty existence with the rugged life of a cavalryman at the front. He also has some interesting comments on General Butler's vigorous conversion of slaves into what he calls "contraband of war," a process Butler pioneered earlier in the war. Frank leaves no doubt as to his attitude toward slavery. Nor does he mince words on the subject of his father's salary!

Leonardtown, Md.
February 14th, 1864
Dear Father,
The receipt of several papers during the past week from home notifies me that you still remember me although I have not received any letters. We have not received any order to leave this <u>*sunny*</u> *and pleasant place yet to go once more into the wilds of Virginia, and take part in another hard and muddy spring campaign with the Army of the Potomac, though we are in monumental expectation of it. It will be rather hard for us, at first. I expect (after a winter of ease and quietness, with good snug, comfortable quarters in a hotel with plenty of good things to eat) to again have to do picket in the front of the army, to make forced marches, and reconnaissances in the mud, sleeping on the ground, with the broad canopy of the heavens above us for our mantle, a saddle for a pillow, and perhaps nothing but a "hardtack" and a piece of salt pork to alleviate our hunger, all of which privations our officers and men, that are unfortunate enough to be with the regiment, have to undergo often this winter. How they will laugh at us when we get back there, and commence our grumbling at the hard fare, and wish ourselves snugly ensconced in our comfortable quarters at Fenwicks Hotel in this place. Any how they will heap the extra duty on our poor devoted heads, and declare that we deserve it, not having done anything all winter. I can imagine it all—. But what has been done once I suppose can be done again by the same parties. I suppose I ought not be call[ing] them unfortunate for being with the regiment, but rather fortunate in being able to do such a good work. And I ought to lament that I am not there to enjoy with them their misery, and*

95

*although I yield to no one in my devotion to the Union
and patriotism, yet I cannot say that I do—Gen'l Butler
is throwing down coals of fire on his head by his energetic
action in this Dept. The secessionists are trembling with
rage, because he is taking all their negroes away from
them. An infantry officer has been here recruiting and
also a cavalry officer, and both together they have taken
away large numbers. The negroes here have the war fever
now. Strong and nearly all the able bodied ones will go
into the army, and the white people who have always
lived upon their labor begin to look about themselves to
see how they are going to live without them. Men who
have never done a day's work will have to this spring, or
else come to poverty, and women who have always lived
in their sitting rooms and parlors in idleness will have to
go into their kitchens and work like our northern ladies
do, great will be the fall thereof but words will certainly
prove true, for the women servants are all leaving as well
as the men. It will be two years before they can recover
from the ruin and decay which slavery has brought upon
them, but eventually they will be much better off for its
abolishment.—*

*The Legislature I see is agitating an increase in the pay
of the Judges, and well may they do so. I consider it
disgraceful for such a noble and first class old state as
Maine to pay her Judges such a niggardly pittance. Why
should justice and talent command so much higher price
in other states, where the labor is not as great? There is no
mistaking it, the people of Maine are slow in their
advance towards a higher order of improvement in
everything. I fear they do not appreciate the worth of the
Supreme Judiciary of the State. They try to be too
economical and in doing so, they fall so far behind the
times, that they have to take a big jump all at once, and
it requires a good deal of agitating and steaming up to
make them do it. (Excuse this rather loose expression; it
sums up my ideas though.) The salaries of the Judges*

The Maine Supreme Judicial Court, circa 1865-1870. Judge Jonathan Dickerson is in the front row, far right. Other Justices are: front, from left — Charles W. Walton, Deering; Jonas Cutting, Bangor; Chief Justice John Appleton, Bangor; Edward Kent, Bangor; back, from left — Rufus P. Tapley, Saco; William G. Barrows, Brunswick; Charles Danforth, Gardiner. (Courtesy Waldo County Law Library)

MICHELE LEACH

97

should have been raised six or eight years ago, but legal talent has stood it so long that I fear the legislature will think that it never ought to be raised. — I believe in economy but not in an economy which surely sooner or later sacrifice[s] the interests of the people, nor in an economy which lays justice at so low a premium and brings the highest judicial tribunal of a state on a par with the police, common, and magistrate courts, of inferior states. In such a State (if the matter is not soon remedied), the Judiciary (in which all the rights and interests of the people are centered) will soon fall into decay and ten cent lawyers and pettifoggers will in a few years be the weighers and measurers of justice to the people, then when it is too late will they see their error, and find out that economy is not bought at such a price. —[3]

I have, as I wrote you in a previous letter, given up all thoughts of coming home this winter, and though I did it reluctantly, I think it is best, for several good reasons. I hope you will not be much disappointed. If I should get a leave while here and the detachment should be ordered away while I was absent, my papers and public properties for which I am responsible would be left in a very unsafe and loose condition, not being able to attend to it myself, and I might get into difficulty. This is only one reason which is a very important one. Capt. Ash of my regiment and several new Com. officers and privates were wounded in the late reconnaissance of the Army of the Potomac, as well as several privates killed. This is the second time Capt. Ash has been wounded, the first time receiving five different wounds—I have this day written Ellen. My love to Mother and Lulu and believe me to be as ever your most affectionate son

Frank W. Dickerson, U.S.C.

Hon. J.G. Dickerson
Belfast, Me.

A Union cavalry raid on Richmond, in two columns, one led by General Judson Kilpatrick, the other by Col. Ulric Dahlgren, was launched from the Rapidan River on February 29. Kilpatrick reached the city's outer fortifications but found them too strong to breach. As he rode east down the Peninsula, Colonel Dahlgren with his five hundred men probed to within two miles of the Confederate capital before being confronted by Rebel cavalry under General Custis Lee and withdrawing. Ambushed as his force retreated, Dahlgren, son of U.S. Navy Admiral John Dahlgren, was killed. The cavalry raid against Richmond failed "despite an auspicious start, through lack of surprise, lack of force, and . . . lack of drive to see it through."[4]

Meanwhile, the 5th U.S. Cavalry took part in a diversionary raid toward Charlottesville as part of a force commanded by the flamboyant 24-year-old Brig. Gen. George Armstrong Custer, formerly of Frank's regiment.

Meanwhile, Lieutenant Dickerson, now stationed at Point Lookout, Maryland, could only experience vicariously the exploits of his regiment.

Head Qurs. Cav'l De't
Point Lookout, Md
March 8, 1864

Dear Father,

I received a letter from you the other day informing me that all was well at home which I was glad to hear. I am again stationed at this place, having returned from Leonardtown some two days ago. I don't like the situation so well as at Leonardtown, though I am very well off here. I suppose I shall return to Leonardtown as soon as the veterans, who have nearly all reenlisted and gone home, return. The late reconnaissance by the Cavalry in our army don't seem to have developed much, though the one made by Gen'l Custer (1 L't of "M" Co. 5th Cav'l) was a brilliant one; as usual the 5th Cav's carried off the plan [palm?], and did most of the fighting.

I presume you saw an account of Capt Ash's movements, the capturing of camp, guns, etc. with only 60 men. The 5th Cav'l has the smartest and proudest name of any regiment of the cavalry in the U.S. Army either. — It has won many cavalry fights, lost more men to the war, and had more officers wounded I almost might say than any two regiments that have been raised and put in the field. And as for discipline, some of the regular regt's are as volunteers compared to them. However, it needs no words of mine to praise it, as its deeds speak for it.

I have had a letter from Ellen since her return relative to the wonderful time she had in Boston, etc. She seems to be very happy in Gt. Barrington. I have no news to recite of any consequence, I think our exchange of prisoners will soon be affected. My love to mother and Lulu. I received a letter from Mother the other day for which please present to her a thousand grateful thanks. I shall answer soon as I can pick up an item or so of excitement.

Affectionately,
Your son
Frank

At the end of March, Frank, now returned to Leonardtown, explains the paucity of recent letters.

Leonardtown, Md.
March 30, 1864

Dear Father,

I have received your several kind letters and papers for which I am very thankful.

I have been sick nearly all of the month. I came to Leonardtown last Sunday, since which time I have been confined to my room. I was so as to be about while at the Point, though really was not able to. — It is my old complaint again, diarrhea, and this time worse than I have ever had it before, even worse than when I was on the Peninsula, as it was attended by a cold and symptoms of fever. I am now slowly recovering and when I receive some attention which was not the case at the Point as I lived in a tent, and wasn't much protected from the inclemency of the weather. I am getting well now however but am still quite weak, expect to be ready for duty again by the middle of next week—This accounts for me not writing oftener lately. Will write again in a day or two. Much love to all at home. Write to me at this place. Affec your son

Frank

Poor health has become a fact of life, with which he deals bravely. The chronic diarrhea will be with him to the end, and Frank develops a nagging cough at Leonardtown which proves especially troublesome.[5]

Leonardtown, Md.
April 10th 1864

Dear Father

I have nothing of importance to record since my last writing you, except that I am very much improved in health and strength, and though I have not yet reported for duty still I trust I am nearly well again. I had quite a siege of it, for six weeks, two weeks of the time being confined to my room—I am now out and sound again almost the same as usual, only not quite regained my strength.

Gen'l Marston has been relieved from the command of this District, Gen'l Hincks having been substituted in his place. — He is quite a young man, has been wounded several times, is from Massachusetts. — Our Command is still retained here, doing some duty as previously. I have not yet seen Gen'l Hincks but understand he is quite

101

popular at the Point—

We have had the most disagreeable weather imaginable here for the last three weeks, constant rains, snow storms etc. I receive the papers you send me quite regularly, and am very thankful for them, this reading affords me a great deal of pleasure.

I heard from Ellen the other day. She is quite happy as usual. — I went down to Fortress Monroe and Norfolk some 3 or 4 weeks ago, and staid 4 or 5 days, had a most pleasant trip. —

Much love to Mother and Lulu and accept some yourself. —

> *I'm your most aff. son*
> *Frank W. Dickerson, U.S.A.*

Hon. J.G. Dickerson
Belfast, Me.

P.S. I have the pleasure to state that Gen'l Grant has selected from out all the cavalry in the army, two companies of the 5th Cavalry for his personal escort and body guard. My friend Capt Mason commands them. This is a great compliment and honor.

> *F.W.D.*

Frank has considerable news to report in his next letter. General Grant had discontinued the prisoner exchange system to weaken the Confederate armies which may have prompted the rumor of a Confederate raid to free Rebel prisoners of war.

> *Head qurs Cav'l Det*
> *District St. Mary's*
> *Leonardtown, Md.*
> *May 3rd, 1864*

Dear Father

I have received your letter dated at Ellsworth—and was glad to learn that your tour there is likely to be a

pleasant one. I am now doing duty again same as ever
again. We have been considerably alarmed here lately at
reports and rumors, which have been in circulation here
to the effect that a large force of the rebels is on the
opposite side of the Potomac, where they have collected a
large number of small boats in which they intend to cross
the river and make a raid on this place and Point
Lookout, with the express intent of liberating their men
(new prisoners of war) at the latter place. It is a daring
scheme and one which seems hardly inditable, still it
might be attempted, but in my opinion with small
prospects of success. — That they could come over in that
way, in considerable force is not to be doubted much, but
the idea of their being able to get back themselves, or that
they could get any plunder, or their prisoners back (even
in the event of their releasing them) seems to me to be an
impossibility. — To affect such an object successfully they
must have a "Ram" to destroy our gunboats stationed
around and in the vicinity of Pt. Lookout, together with
one or two transports to carry away their released
soldiers and their booty which would be very large,
should they take the Point. — But this they are not going
to attempt at a risk followed by such consequences as it
inevitably would be, especially at a time when all of their
army in Virginia is watching the movements of Grant. —
However, should they attempt such a foolhardy
movement, we have made arrangements to give them a
fitting reception. — The Point is strongly guarded with
troops and defended by stockades, etc. which they would
first have to break through, and we have scouts and
detached parties throughout all parts who are on the alert
and would no doubt have ample opportunity to give us
timely warning. Within the last two days, we have
scouted through the whole country. I was out with one
party all Sunday night, and all day Monday. — This
was made necessary by the report that Gen'l Fitzhugh Lee
had several officers over here in citizens dress, making

*observations, and arrangements for the portended
movement. I did not, neither did any of the other parties
that were out, discover anything to substantiate that
report. — We had every arrangement made on Sunday
night to burn our camp and all our Ordnance,
Quartermaster and Commissary stores in case they
should come in such force as to prevent our being able to
defend it and hold it—The rebels on the other side are
very much exasperated at the two very successful raids we
have made on them and would no doubt hazard a good
deal to retaliate. — But we have no fears at all of the
result if they attempt the proposed scheme, which will
burst like a bubble before their disappointed visions after
they get over here. — A rocket thrown up from this place
would bring two or three gunboats up to the mouth of-
head-of the bay (Potomac) and then "Mr. Johnny" you
can bid farewell to Dixie for some time. I have written
considerable on this subject as it is one which has been
the all absorbing subject of discussion and conversation
both here and at Point Lookout for sometime past, and
more especially at Point Lookout where they have been
stampeded several nights lately by false alarms. — It has
also caused our cavalry a deal of extra hard work for a
week past—Now I want to get your opinion on a legal
question. My friend and brother officer Lieut Denney is
the recruiting officer of the Detachment. He reenlisted
some 50 men of the Detachment. They were credited to the
quota of the State of New Jersey. That state paying them a
bounty of $300.00 cash down on enlistment for so doing,
this being additional to the bounty given them by the
general government which is $402.00. When the agent of
the state came down here to pay these bounties, he found
he had not brought finances enough with him to pay them
all, so he went back to Washington for the balance which
was due. After getting there, he concluded he would not
come down again himself, but wrote Lieut Denney that
he had deposited $3,000.00 in the First National Bank*

of Washington, subject to his (Lieut Denney's order) and that his checks on that bank would be cashed provided he sent a copy of each man's enlistment to the bank with the checks—Lieut. Denney, supposing as we all did that everything was all right, complied with his letter,— sending copies of each man's enlistment to the "Bank" of W and issuing the checks on the account of the State Agent, and signing them himself. Lieut D showed the letter he had received from the State Agent authorizing him to issue the check to a banker here in town, who, being satisfied that everything was right cashed the check for the men and sent them on to the bank, where they were refused payment, the ground that there was no money on deposit to the credit of the State Agent. — The enlistment papers had been duly received and even acknowledged. Neither were they returned to Lieut D [who] is liable to the banker for the amt of the checks cashed and also if under the circumstances he can be held accountable to the civil law for any offense, and if so what the nature of the offense is. I hope it will be satisfactorily arranged and think it will—Lieut D has all the letters, etc. he had received relative to the case in his possession. I know that so far as he is concerned he is perfectly innocent, and everything that he did was done in good faith, and for the interest of the service and the benefit of the State of New Jersey—and knowing this, should he be amenable to civil law and liable to arrest, and should the banker here attempt to have him arrested by civil authorities, I shall not permit them to do it, until I have submitted the whole case to Major Gen'l Butler, for his instructions thereon. I hope you understand my rather indefinite explanation of the case and will favor me with an early reply.

What do you think of my letter to the proprietor and Editor of St. Mary's Gazette? A copy of which I sent to Mother. I see it is extensively copied into the papers, and wouldn't wonder much if it should creep into some of the

Congressional debates soon. — My love to Mother and Lulu—

As ever affectionately your son
Frank W. Dickerson

Hon. J.G. Dickerson
Belfast, Me.

The hard luck boys of the Army of the Potomac first saw their new general-in-chief as he reviewed them with his Maine-born friend Congressman Elihu Washburne of Illinois. They took one look at the black-suited politician and decided Grant was taking his own undertaker along!

On May 4, the vast army crossed the Rappahannock River and entered the Wilderness of evil memory. Grant planned to push quickly through this impossible terrain and fight Lee in the open country on the other side. But the relentless Virginian hit him with everything he had. Of the Battle of the Wilderness one soldier said it was a fight "no man saw or could see." Another dubbed it "a battle of invisibles with invisibles." A third commented, "As for fighting, it was simply bushwhacking on a grand scale, in brush where all formation beyond that of regiments or companies was soon lost and where such a thing as a constant line of battle on either side was impossible." As at Chancellorsville, the woods caught on fire, and troops of both sides groped blindly through black powder and wood smoke, and tried, often unsuccessfully, to rescue the shrieking wounded from the flames. At one crucial point in the battle, General Lee, with flushed face and flashing eyes, spurred forward his gray war-horse "Traveller" to lead a Rebel contingent into battle, whereupon the troops halted in their tracks and shouted, "Lee to the rear!" They knew that to lose Lee was to lose the war. The General reluctantly complied.[6]

This gruesome battle (May 5-6) cost the Union 17,666 casualties out of a total of 101,895 engaged, with 2,246 killed. The Confederates suffered an estimated 7,750 casualties out of an estimated effective strength of 61,025.

At the end of the Wilderness fight, General Grant flung himself on his cot and wept. Then he got up and prepared for the next stage of the campaign. When the troops saw the General and his staff galloping south, they cheered as they had not cheered a general since McClellan's day. No humiliating retreat as so often in the past! Gratefully they followed him toward Spotsylvania, as Grant sidled southward to slip around Lee's right flank. Fighting of unparalleled ferocity ensued in the series of battles of the Spotsylvania campaign (May 8-21) with Federal casualties of 17,500 out of 110,000 engaged and heavy Confederate losses (the number not definitively recorded) out of some 50,000 engaged.

Meanwhile, "Fighting Phil" Sheridan, commander of the Army of the Potomac cavalry, had launched another raid toward Richmond, with Frank's regiment among his 10,000 troopers. On May 11, in a hot skirmish at Yellow Tavern, a Michigan trooper mortally wounded Jeb Stuart, an irreparable loss to the Army of Northern Virginia. The results of the raid:

> In his first independent cavalry action Sheridan had ridden completely around Lee's army, had destroyed vital supplies and communications, had beaten the Confederates in four engagements, and had then extricated himself from a dangerous situation.[7]

Leonardtown, Md.
May 19th, 1864

Dear Father,

Yours of the 13th is just received. I was glad to hear that all are well at home. Nothing new here. We are all awaiting with anxiety to hear the latest from Gen'l Grant. Everything so far looks favorable, and though all our gains have been purchased at a great cost, still it is the only way we can end the war. If McClellan had been in command of the army during this campaign, he would have retired across the Rapidan after the fight at the Wilderness to reorganize, which would have taken six months. Capt. Ash of my regiment, whose gallantry is proverbial in the army, has been killed. Also Lieut

*Sweetman, killed while leading a charge at Yellow
Tavern. Lieut Wilson is wounded. I have received no
particulars of Capt. Ash's death. — These are the only
casualties I have as yet seen reported, have not received
any letters from the regiment since the campaign
commenced. — Gen'l Custer of my regiment (a 1st Lieut)
[in the Regular Army] has done nobly I see by the papers.
I am anxious to hear the result of Gen'l Butler's
operations. I have fears in relation to his command,
nothing having been heard from him for several days.*

*I should like to see a copy of the "Whig" containing a
notice of our request to editor Gay. I believe I have a pair
of white pants at home, if so can you send them to me by
express? Direct them as follows and I shall no doubt
receive them all right. —*

Lieutenant F.W. Dickerson, U.S.A.
Baltimore, Md.
My love to all at home,

> *In haste,*
> *Your affec. Son*
> *F.W. Dickerson*

June, 1864, proved an eventful month in the Civil War. On June
3, Grant hurled masses of troops at Lee's entrenched Confederates at Cold Harbor and in one frightful fight of less than an
hour, Army of the Potomac killed and wounded numbered a stag-
gering 7,000, to some 1,500 Army of Northern Virginia boys. The
Union army still heavily outnumbered the Confederate army, and
soon General Grant's mighty host would cross the James River on
a mammoth pontoon bridge.

On June 8, the National Union Party (the Republican Party in
wartime guise) convention had renominated President Lincoln
overwhelmingly but had substituted Military Governor Andrew
Johnson of Tennessee for Judge Dickerson's old friend, incum-
bent Vice President Hannibal Hamlin of Bangor, Maine, as Lincoln's running mate.

Frank continues to root out the disloyal, including some of the "female sex". His faith in General Grant remains unabated.

Leonardtown, Md.
June 14th, 1864
Dear Father,
It seems a long time since I have heard from you, though I suppose it may arise from the fact that you are away from home, or perhaps otherwise busily engaged. —
I am still moving about in this vicinity in the even [tenor?] of my way enforcing the laws among the disloyal and running the governmental machine in the upper part of this county—arresting deserters from the Army of the Potomac (of which there are many) as well also as deserters from the rebel army, carrying out the confiscation decrees, (several estates having been confiscated in this county at our instance), attending to the duties usually connected with a military command, and almost everything else which we think ought to be differently regulated. — Lieut Denney with 50 men went over to Virginia on a raid and has not yet returned, will probably be two or three days longer. I was at Point Lookout when he left, having been summoned there as a witness before a military commission for the trial of citizens. Lieut Mix, commanding the cavalry of the District, was also sick and unable to go, so he [Lt. Denney] was obliged to go alone.
We have created great consternation here lately among the citizens by arresting many prominent ones and sending them to Point Lookout for trial by the Commission, the female sex being included in some cases as well as the males. Some of these people have already been sent to the Rip-Raps to reflect upon the fruits of their disloyalty.
The latest news from Grant still is encouraging, and though not developing or showing much activity, except

109

cavalry operation, still my confidence in him does not yet abate one jot or tittle. And I am firmly convinced as ever of his ability and will to take Richmond. —

I trust all are well and comfortable at home, and hope I may have an opportunity of seeing you all sometime during the summer or fall.

With much love to all at home I am as ever
                              Your affectionate son
                              F. W. Dickerson

Hon. J. G. Dickerson
Belfast, Maine

P.S. Accept many thanks for newspapers.
          Frank

By the time Frank wrote his next letter, the Army of the Potomac had failed to breach the Confederate lines shielding Petersburg just south of Richmond and had settled in for a long siege. On June 19, the U.S. Navy scored a great triumph when the U.S.S. *Kearsarge* sank the C.S.S. *Alabama*, the South's most dreaded commerce destroyer, off Cherbourg, France. And in the Western theater, General Sherman, the very personification of the implacability of total war, drove Joe Johnston's army ever closer to Atlanta. Unfortunately, Frank's health continued precarious, although he bravely reports a slight improvement.

                    Leonardtown, Md.
                    June 26th 1864
Dear Father,
   I received your letter of a recent date enclosing photograph of Lulu which I consider excellent.
   I have applied for a leave of absence of 30 days on account of my health not being very good, I being unable to stand the hot weather of this climate during this season. I do not have much hope of getting it, however.

— *I have also written to Mr. Merrill [sic] [U.S. Senator Lot M. Morrill of Maine] requesting him to get me ordered on Recruiting or some other light duty in some one of the N.E. States either Maine, New Hampshire, or Mass. My health, though better than it was when confined to my room, is by no means strong enough to endure the duties required of me in this climate. I am determined to make every effort possible to get away from here. Though not able to be about, most of the time I am on duty. —Still I feel miserable all the time. And I do not improve as I ought to after a sickness. —*

I wish you would write to Mr. Merrill and Mr. Hamlin [Hannibal Hamlin of Maine, Vice President of the United States, 1861-65] on this subject and, as this command is now incorporated into the Dept of Washington, I have no doubt but what they can effect my wish. Everything remains same as ever here. We are now having the hottest weather that I ever experienced. Completely melting and enervating. —

I shall not probably hear from my leave of absence under 10 days as I only sent it in a day or two since. — My love to all at home. Hope I shall be able to see you in the course of a fortnight or three weeks. —

> *As ever Affect*
> *Your son*
> *Frank*

Hon. J.G. Dickerson
Belfast

Now a patient at Hammond General Hospital in Point Lookout, Frank "anxiously and hopefully" awaits news that his application for leave of absence had been granted.

Hammond Gen'l Hosp'l
Point Lookout, Md
July 10th 1864

Dear Father

I am situated at present the same as at last writing [Ed. Note: cited letter missing], a patient in this hospital, anxiously and hopefully awaiting the return of my application for leave of absence. —

I am able to be up and about every day, and with the quiet nursing and kind attention I have received I think I am somewhat improved. The sea bathing which I also indulge in once a day I think has also a beneficial effect. — Still under all these favorable circumstances the thoughts of home are uppermost in my mind and my wish to get there grows stronger every day. My application ought to be back either by Tuesday or Wednesday of this week, whether approved or not, in the event of being the former case I shall immediately (if able) proceed on my journey. — I shall make the trip by slow stages and as easily as I can under the circumstances. I intend remaining a day or two in Baltimore with Capt. Leib of my regiment who is there on mustering duty and also to stop a day or two in New York with Lieuts Urban, and Albert White and perhaps a day in Boston, so it will probably be a week after I leave here before I reach home. All this of course depends on the success of my application. If unsuccessful, why I must do the best I can here. The surgeons say I will get well here, but believe I ought to go North where I can get better much sooner and do me also much more good. — The days pass very slowly here although I enjoy the evenings in the society of Dr. Gardener and family most pleasantly. The Doctors are both regular officers, the former the Medical Director and Surgeon in Chief and the other the Executive Officer, and I being the only regular officer here, of course they have some sympathy for me. —

My love to all at home —
Very affectionately
Your Son
Frank

Hon. J.G. Dickerson
Belfast

Meanwhile, the war ground on relentlessly. The Shenandoah Valley campaign began badly for the Union. The Confederates whipped two inept federal commanders in succession. Then the Valley army, reinforced by Lee's Second Corps and commanded by Maj. Gen. Jubal Early, marched on Washington and managed to penetrate as far as Fort Stevens, dangerously close to the White House. There, on July 12, a young Massachusetts Captain named Oliver Wendell Holmes, Jr.[8] spied a tall civilian perilously exposed above the fort's parapet, observing Civil War fighting for the first time. "Get down, you damn fool, before you get shot," the young officer shouted, failing to recognize the President of the United States.[9] The commander-in-chief good-naturedly complied.

Early's small army withdrew, but his amazing feat prompted General Grant to turn the Valley Campaign over to Maj. Gen. Philip H. Sheridan. The little bandy-legged, dark-complexioned Irish-American had a ruthless streak in his makeup that suited him well in the Valley campaign. Commanding infantry, cavalry and artillery, he climaxed hard fighting with a smashing October victory at Cedar Creek, then ravaged the Shenandoah Valley so industriously that, as he boasted, a crow would have to carry its own rations as it soared over what had once been the Confederacy's breadbasket.

On July 14, Frank wrote to Judge Dickerson from the hospital.

I wrote you a few days ago that I expected to hear from my application for leave by Tuesday or Wednesday of this week. But Thursday (today) has already come round and I have heard nothing from it. —and do not expect to until

after the rebel raid of Baltimore and Washington is over. I
suppose all other business except such as pertains to that is
then thrown one side. My health remains about the same,
still am able to be up and walk about a part of each day.

You must not have too strong hopes of my coming home
as I have little faith in my application being approved. I
don't think there is any prospect of my hearing from it
under another week. —

Nothing new here.

But three days later Frank's leave of absence is granted and he
heads for home.

> *Hammond Gen'l Hospital*
> *Point Lookout, Md*
> *July 17th, 1864*

Dear Father

My application for Leave of Absence has finally been
approved. And I shall probably leave tonight or
tomorrow night on my journey home. Shall probably stop
at Portland a few days with you, previous to going down
home. Expect to reach Portland by Friday or Saturday.
— Expect to remain a day in Baltimore, a day in New
York and a day in Boston. Will probably stop at the
American House in Boston. —

> *Affectionately your son*
> *Frank*

While Frank recuperated in Belfast, General Sherman's armies
battered at the Army of Tennessee, commanded now by General
John B. Hood, a fierce fighter with, as one observer noted,
a lion's heart but a head of wood! A tawny beard covered Hood's
long, rather sad face, and he had lost a leg (he had to be strapped
into the saddle) and the full use of an arm in battle, but his jugular instinct remained intact. He repeatedly hurled his weary,

diminishing ranks at Sherman, only to be bloodily repulsed each time. On September 2, Atlanta fell, and Grant saluted this great victory—as he did all his subordinates' triumphs—by firing a 100-gun salute directly into the Rebel lines at Petersburg.

Sherman now pondered his next move. With Grant's reluctant permission (he felt Sherman should finish off Hood), General Sherman prepared to slash down through the heart of Georgia "from Atlanta to the sea" with over 60,000 men on a wide front. He set out in mid-November. "I propose to demonstrate the vulnerability of the South and make its inhabitants feel that war and individual ruin are synonymous terms," he explained to General George H. Thomas, left behind with the balance of the army to deal with Hood.[10]

Sherman proved as good as his word. He severed his supply-line and foraged liberally off the land, bringing the war home with a vengeance to Georgia civilians. Tragically, houses were burned and property destroyed, and the message came across loud and clear to the people of the state: bluecoat armies could now roam at will in the South, burning and pillaging with the Confederate government powerless to stop them. By the time Sherman reached Savannah and the sea in December, his gorged troops could scarcely stomach another plump goose, fat turkey or succulent ham. They returned to their hardtack and salt pork with a feeling of relief.

But the march through Georgia lay in the future as Frank wrote to his father in Dover, Maine, from Belfast on September 17 to inform him that when his leave ended, he had been ordered to report to General Grant's headquarters at City Point.

This is quite an honor as it brings me on the staff of Gen'l Grant, and also, as I understand it, an easy position. I have written Capt. Mason telling him that I had intended to report to Annapolis previous to receiving his offer, also informing him about my health, that I might not be able at first to perform all the duties he would expect and require, that I might get sick again and have to leave him after being with him only a short time, and not having been of much service to him, that my being able to stay in the field is only

115

*an experiment, and that if he is willing to take me, knowing
these facts I will gladly accept his offer. — He will write me at
Baltimore letting me know [in] season to report to Annapolis,
or to him before my "leave" runs out. — I have made up my
mind if he concludes to accept me, to go to the Head Qurts of
the Army, and, if not, to Annapolis, and in case I am not able
to perform the duties required of me at the former place, I can
then go to the latter. — We are all well at home. I expect to go
Thursday and hope you may get back before that time. —
All my love—*

His next letter is from Baltimore.

*Baltimore
Sept 27th 1864*

Dear Father

*I arrived here yesterday morn. (Monday) from Phila
where I remained on Sunday. . . . My health is really
better I think than when I left home—The journey
considerably fatigued me—but I had a good long rest in
Phila—I intend leaving for the army either tonight or
tomorrow night.—I called on Ellen in Boston and found
her most happily comfortable and satisfactorily situated.
I will write you after I arrive in the army giving fuller
accounts of my visit in Boston and Phila. I only write
now to inform you I am well.*

*Direct to me as follows: Lieut F. W. Dickerson, 5th U.S.
Cavl'y, HeadQurs, Armies of the U.S. City Point Va.*

*Love to Mother and to Lulu
Affectionately
Frank*

Frank arrived at City Point on September 29.

I found my friend Capt. Mason awaited my arrival at the wharf, and apparently glad to see me. — The camp of our command is a most excellent one, and the opportunities and advantages of being at Head Quarters Armies of the U.S. are everywhere made manifest. — Our tents are all floored as are also those of the men—and we also have a house made of boards for mess quarters. — Capt M has four officers with him, myself and Lieuts Raur, Churchill and Taylor. Our own H'd Qurs. are about as far from Gen'l Grant's as from our house to Mr. Twingel's. I have not seen the Gen'l but once, and then in the evening at a distance, so I couldn't form much of an idea of his personal appearance, this subject will have to be reserved for a later letter. The evening I arrived the Gen'l was up the river superintending the late fight of Gen'l Butler's army, he went up and came back on a steamer accompanied by his staff and a few orderlies. — We could hear the commanding and at times the musketry very distinctly from our camp. You have already, I suppose, received the accounts of the late operations from the newspapers, which do not vary much the accounts we have. — The Army of the Potomac have been engaged in fighting at different points along the line, and have been successful. — Everybody is in good spirits at H'd Qur's— and an officer of the staff who has just left my tent says he thinks Richmond will be ours in a fortnight. — Gen'l Meade's H'd Qurs are about 8 miles from here. — I have not been up as yet to the army or visited any part of our line, and can give you no description of its appearance form my own observation. I can only tell you that this army is at work and that we are in the [midst of] very exciting events. A violent rain storm has been prevailing all day long, which I fear may retard movements somewhat—I understand that the Gen'l rarely takes out the whole escort and the evidences are that the duty is light. My call upon Ellen in Boston was a very pleasant and interesting one. Mr. & Mrs. Gannet I found very pleasant and Mr. G. showed me the school, gymnasium etc. Ellen appeared happy and contented—and

*well she might as she seemed to be surrounded by all the
comforts of a cultivated and luxurious home.— . . . . My
health I think is better than when I left home, and if the
duties are no more arduous than what I have reason to
believe they are and I do not get any worse I think I shall be
able to get along. I shall write again soon—With much love
to Mother, LuLu and yourself.*

His next letter is directed to his mother and describes what it is
like at headquarters.

*HeadQurs Det 5th Cavalry
City Point, Va.
October 9th 1864*

Dear Mother,

*I received your letter of a recent date last evening and
as the first from home since I left I welcome it heartily. —
I am sorry that I have so little to chronicle of interest in
return. — You will no doubt be quite surprised when I
tell you that I have not seen the Lieutenant General
(Grant) in the face yet, though his quarters are but a
stones throw from mine. I suppose I might have seen him
if I had the curiosity to watch for the opportunity. He has
been away to Washington and elsewhere for the past three
or four days, returning this evening. — Capt. Mason also
went away to Washington on leave of six days last
Tuesday and has not yet returned. During his absence I
have been in command of the escort and have so far had
literally nothing to do—The whole escort has not been
out but once since I came, and it then went out on an
independent scout under Capt. M[ason] — I remain
in charge of camp. I have made several agreeable
acquaintances among the officers of the Gen'l Staff—
officers of the highest ability and talent. General Grant's
staff is very small, only 7 or 8 officers, while General
Meade has nearly 50. Head Qurs. does not occupy more*

than a dozen tents and has only 14 wagons for their transportation while Gen'l Meade's Head Qur's. train consists of nearly 120 wagons. — Gen'l G__ lives in a larger hospital tent in the same line with his staff and also messes with them. It is very quiet here indeed and you would scarcely imagine that here it is where all the plans for the movements, confrontations and operations of our army first emanate. Below us down by the river all is business, noise, bustle, life and confusion. This is the great base of supplies for the army, immense store houses, wharfs and piers extend along the bank of the river for an incredible distance all connected with each other. The wharves are lined with steamers and barges, and sailing vessels unloading every conceivable kind of stores, supplies, equipments, and munitions of war. The river itself is dotted with transports and steamers, continually passing to and fro, and there would seem to be no end to the immense amount of business transacted, and yet the beauty of all is the method and system with which it is all done. Every Department has its wharves, its store houses, its guards, its decks and its employees. — On the land behind, close to the wharf, is the City Point and Petersburg R.R. by which all those supplies are carried up to the Army of the Potomac—trains running day and night and the shrill whistle and the ringing of the bells is incessant. Settlers, Squatters, and vendors of almost anything, have lined the road along the R.R. and wharves with their huts, shanties and tents. — Not many roads back of all this, but many feet higher, (and though close by, yet out of sight) on a long level lawn well interspersed with trees with a view for miles both up and down the river, lays the camp of the 5th Cavl and 4th Infantry, Gen'l Grant's old regiment which does guard duty for Hd Qurs. —

I rode out some 12 or 13 miles for pleasure the other day without feeling any worse for it. My health I think is better than when I left home, and as yet do not regret coming.

119

Gen'l Meade's H'd Quarters are some 14 miles from here, and Gen'l Hancock's are some 6 miles from there, so I am afraid I shall not have an opportunity of seeing Ansel White very soon. — You must all write often. Give my love to father and LuLu and believe me to be as ever yours affectionately

Frank

Frank's next two letters note continuing health problems although, characteristically, he tries to remain optimistic:

City Point, Va.
October 23rd, 1864

Dear Father

You may be somewhat surprised, (though you need not be ashamed) to learn that I have received another "Leave of Absence" on account of sickness—of 20 days. — The trouble is with my cough which continues to hold and is now accompanied by a severe and rather painful hoarseness—I have not been able to speak in a natural tone for the last ten days. Capt Mason and our doctor thought I better go away for a short time under medical treatment. So I expect to go to Washington tomorrow morning when I shall report to Dr. Vanis, an old army surgeon for medical treatment, and probably remain there or at Baltimore under some surgeon's treatment until I am better. In all probability I shall go upon some light duty at the expiration of my leave. — In some other respects I am better than when I left home, stronger and heartier. — In all probability a great battle will be fought by this army within the next ten days, perhaps it will commence before you receive this letter.[11] — Genl's Meade and Butler have been here all the afternoon and evening in consultation with General Grant, and all the Corps Commanders of the Potomac army even in

*consultation with General Meade. This morning I have
heard that one corps of the Army of the James is to
reinforce the Potomac Army. Every indication points
to an early move. I will write you where to direct your
letters. Love to Mother and LuLu.*

> *Affectionately*
> *Your son*
> *F.W. Dickerson*
> *Lt. 5th Cav'y*

◆

> *Baltimore, Md*
> *October 28th 1864*

Dear Father

*I arrived here last Thursday evening and reported the
next morning to Dr. Hanson an old army surgeon for
medical treatment. I am boarding with Capt. Leib of
my regt who is here on duty. My cough is not near as
troublesome as when I left home but seems to have wound
up with a severe bronchial affection, which I suppose was
caused by exposure at City Point. — I was very loth to
leave Gen. Grants H'd Qur's and only because I was
advised by Capt. Mason and other friends. I shall
probably go on some light duty at the expiration of my
leave either in this city or some other city where the
climate is favorable for my disease. Capt. Mason is very
popular at H'd Qur's and can get almost anything done
that he wants. He felt sorry that he had me detailed with
him as I had to come away, and seemed (though without
any reason as he did it for my good) to blame himself for
it. — He and other friends in high places will see that I
get a good position wherever I want it—I have no fears of
[not] being well looked out for. I should like very much to
hear from you, not having received a letter since I left
home from you, though I have written several— My love*

121

to Mother and LuLu and accept much yourself from your
aff. son.

Frank

"The election is of course the all engrossing subject conversation now," Frank wrote his father from Baltimore on October 31. The Democratic National Convention, meeting in Chicago late in August, had nominated Frank's old commander General George B. McClellan for President and George H. Pendelton of Ohio for Vice President on a platform harshly critical of the Administration and its conduct of the war. It asserted that

> justice, humanity, liberty and the public welfare demand that immediate efforts be made for a cessation of hostilities, with a view to an ultimate convention of the States, or other peaceable means, to the end that at the earliest practicable moment peace may be restored on the basis of the Federal Union of the States.

McClellan accepted the nomination but rejected the peace provision, stating that since "The Union is the one condition of peace," the war must go on until the Union was restored.[12] McClellan believed his endorsement of the "peace plank" would represent a betrayal of his soldiers who have fought and died for the sacred Union.

Little Mac's principled tinkering with the Democratic platform failed to convert Frank to his cause, as he notes in this excerpt from a letter dated October 31.

I found out when I was down to the army that Mr.
McClellan wouldn't even get a respectable vote then, and
much to my surprise that very few regular officers are for
him. The army has no desire to see the destinies of the
country in the hands of a Pendleton, a Vallandigham, a
Ling or a Hurd under whom the independence of the South
would soon be recognized, but they wish to see the rebellion
crushed out and accordingly will vote for Lincoln. The great
hopes of the rebels are now centered in Lee's army and the

*desire for McClellan's election, knowing that if he is elected
their speedy acknowledgement is almost certain; on the
other hand they see in the election of Lincoln 4 years more of
war staring them in the face, if they do not yield,—but I
presume there is not much doubt in the mind of any man
but what Lincoln will be reelected. I do not know what your
political principles now are, not having heard from you
since I left home, but if there should be any chance for me to
vote in this city or in Washington with any Maine soldiers,
I shall go to the polls and vote for Lincoln.*

In that same letter, Frank tries to reassure his family about his
health. "I have not as yet been long enough under medical treatment to show much sign of improvement, though I have great
confidence in my physician."

On November 8, Lincoln defeated McClellan by an electoral
vote of 212 to 21, with the President receiving 55% of the popular vote. Frank rejoices, although Lincoln is far from his ideal.

*Baltimore, Md.
Nov 11th 1864*

Dear Father,

*I have the pleasure to acknowledge the receipt of three
letters from you all of different dates, two of which were
forwarded from City Point.*

*I was sorry to learn of Mother's and LuLu's illness but
hope by this time they have both recovered. My own
health in some respects is improving, while in others I am
happy to say it is no worse—. I am much stronger and
fleshier than when at home, and though I do not think my
cough is as bad as when I left home, it still hangs on and
is attended by a severe hoarseness or bronchial affection
which at the time threatened me with loss of voice. I do
not think the climate of Maine would agree with me at all
in my present condition, otherwise I should most
certainly have gone home ere this—*

I expect to go to Washington tomorrow to see about getting light duty in this city or some other favorable locality, would go to California or Oregon if they will send me.

What think you of the election results, aren't they overwhelmingly conclusive of the fact that this is the peoples' war?—I thank God that the result is as it is— is the heaviest blow the rebels have received in a long time. The President's speeches since his reelection are in the true spirit and the most appropriate ones he has ever made. But you have eschewed politics so I refrain from further expressions. — My love to all at home Mother LuLu and yourself—

Frank

Frank's next letter includes an optimistic health report.

Baltimore, Md.
Nov. 18th 1864

Dear Father

I have been within a day or two the happy recipient of a letter from you and one from mother, and I am very glad to inform you in return that my health has improved considerably since my last letter, my hoarseness being better, my cough at least no worse, and my general health very good. My appetite never was known to fail me and in flesh and strength and general health, I think I am ten per cent better off than at home. The cough is the great bug bear now and this is considerably improved since then—I am daily expecting orders for light duty either here or elsewhere. Col. Powers, the Act'g Ass't Provost Marshall Gen'l for this state and Delaware, has applied to the War Dept for me as a Mustering Officer in his Dept, but has heard nothing from it as yet. — I may have to go to Annapolis and be recommended by a board of officers for light duty before I attain it. —

I was not much surprised to learn that you were away from home on election day. It was rather unfortunate that it should happen so, as many people might consider it intentional.

I had no opportunities offered me to vote, if I had I should have availed myself of this privilege and give "old Abe" my vote. He is not a man of my choice by any means, still he was the only choice that all good and loyal men had. McClellan's weak and vacillating character (including want of firmness and decision as shown in his military and political career) in the hands of his party leaders would soon become moulded to theirs and the result of this election would have been a speedy recognition of the South. By the election of Mr. Lincoln, however, we shall have totally different results. The Copperheads[13] *are annihilated and the war will now be carried on with more vigor than ever, instead of believing that the country is fast tending toward anarchy [&] despotism. I believe that the sky of our political horizon is growing brighter and lighter each day. I see no cause for despair or lamentation in the present aspect of affairs. —*

My love to Mother and LuLu and accept much for yourself.

Your son   Frank

The same month the North gave President Lincoln a resounding vote of confidence, a contingent of the army of General George H. Thomas, the burly grey-bearded soldier known to his troops as "Pap" and to history as the "Rock of Chickamauga," took on General Hood's depleted Army of Tennessee. In the Battle of Franklin, Tennessee, entrenched bluecoats massacred charging Rebels, with Confederate casualties at 6,252 men and five dead generals laid side by side on the porch of a house near the battlefield. Then, on December 15 and 16, "Pap" Thomas descended on Hood like an avalanche. The Battle of Nashville resulted in the most complete defeat of any army in the whole war, and Grant once more exultingly saluted the Confederate defenses at Petersburg with projectiles from 100 guns.

Frank spent a quiet Thanksgiving Day in Baltimore.

Baltimore, Md.

Nov. 25th, 1864

Dear Father

I have nothing new to communicate since my last except to inform you that I believe I am gradually improving in my health, which is some consolation to me I assure you. —

Capt Leib has been relieved from duty here and ordered to the regiment which is in the Shenandoah Valley. — I shall probably remain here some ten days longer, and if in the meantime I do not receive any orders for light duty, shall then go to Annapolis, and go before the board of examination of sick officers, and get on duty from there.

I shall not in all probability be able to go back to the field this winter.

Thanksgiving day passed off very quietly with me in this city yesterday. I went to the opera last evening and enjoyed it very much—I suppose you went to Searsport as usual—

Direct your next letter to me at Barnum's Hotel. I shall be more likely to get it there than anywhere else. I had two letters, one from Ellen and one from you, that remained in the Post Office until advertised. Love to all at home.

Affec. Your Son Frank

Frank's next letter speaks of tense days in Belfast, with citizens, including his own father, arming themselves with pistols. Two incidents, both war related, had roiled the usually placid surface of the little city by the bay.

A Belfast scene (artist unknown), circa 1850, showing High Street looking north and Spring Street at the right. The rendering is done on black emery paper, with all but the black and gray portions achieved by scratching away the emery particles with a pen knife. (Collection of Belfast Free Library)

In June, Belfast Police Chief Charles O. McKenney had been seriously wounded in a confrontation with Isaac Grant, a deserter from a Massachusetts regiment and his confederate Charles Knowles, a 7th Maine Regiment deserter. They had stolen two horses and wagons, selling one set to a bona fide purchaser in Belfast, who learned he had been robbed and set the law on the trail of the criminals. McKenney's wounding electrified Belfast, indeed all Waldo County. A spectacular shoot-out between a posse and Grant and Knowles ended with a posse member shot dead, another seriously wounded and Grant, hit by a pistol bullet, fighting on until clubbed to death. Knowles died next day of a fractured skull.

And in October, Waldo County Deputy Sheriff David W. Edwards attempted to serve a draft notice on a hard-case named Day and died of a bullet through the forehead.

Baltimore, Md.
Dec 5th 1864

Dear Father

I received your favor of a recent date with much pleasure—Am always glad to hear that all are well and happy at home—It is indeed encouraging to receive a letter from home filled with good news from home and to know that they at least are enjoying life's greatest blessing. — God grant that such a state of things may continue—long time uninterrupted. It has been very lonesome here for the past week since Capt. Leib left. — I have heard nothing further from my application for light duty and I expect to leave tomorrow for Annapolis to go into the officers hospital awhile for treatment and from there I expect to get my orders.

I received a long letter from Ellen giving me a glowing account of your visit to Boston, what you did and saw together and last though not least a description of her beautiful furs etc. She seems very happy and I hope she will improve correspondingly. — The Thanksgiving dinner that I partook of, though very excellent, didn't taste like the good old fashioned Searsport Thanksgiving dinners of former years. The last three of which I have been unfortunate enough to miss.

I think this war must have fearfully demoralized Belfast from all accounts, at least when peaceable citizens are obliged to keep revolvers for self protection, a thing unheard of in my day at home. I think your revolver is the first war like weapon ever introduced by you into the house. I trust you may never have occasion to use it; my health was once more restored and I will do all the fighting for the family. That is necessary to be done. The situation of affairs now looks favorable to me. Look out for heavy fighting in the Potomac around the year end. The sixth corps has returned to the Army of the Potomac. I enclose you a couple of photographs taken recently — I hope you will like them. If so I will send down you some more for distribution among my friends.

My health is about the same as at last writing, no worse. I have not recovered my voice yet, though I think it is much stronger and better than when I came home. My love to Mother, will write her soon, also the same and a Kiss for LuLu. Please direct your mail to Annapolis, Md.
Your son, Frank

Frank's health has now, in less than a month, reached the point where the most he can hope for is "light duty", the worst-case scenario being retirement, as he explains in his December 9 letter.

I arrived [at Annapolis] on the evening of the 6th and reported the following morning. — There are three other officers in the room with me, two Captains of the regular infantry and a Swedish officer. Our quarters are very comfortable as we occupy one of the buildings formerly used by the naval cadets as well as the officers quarters are now used for an officers hospital. Yesterday I appeared before the board of examiners of which Gen'l Graham is President.

129

Of course I do not as yet know what will be the result. It is possible they may want to retire me, but this I will not consent to. Preferring to resign, for when I leave the army I want to leave it altogether and be free from it and not trammelled by a retirement, but this [is] only an extreme view of the case. But it is well to look every contingency squarely in the face in the beginning. I trust though that the board will recommend me for light duty.

Eighteen sixty-four had come to a close, with the forces of the Union within striking distance of victory. Sadly, Frank Dickerson's future prospects seem less promising. But still he has hopes.

Annapolis, Md.
Dec. 25, 1864

Dear Father

I received your letter informing me of your arrival in Portland a few days since, and should have answered it before had I anything of importance to record, as it is I only write to inform you that I remain in status quo, and no very speedy prospects of a change. There are officers here who have been here over two months, during which time they have been able for light duty, but cannot get it—I have very comfortable quarters and am associated with officers of the regular service, Lieut. Mix who was with me at Leonardtown is here, not having recovered from his wound—he is also a candidate for light duty. — I wrote to Mr. Merrill [sic] in regards to my case some two days ago but have not as yet received any reply—I shall wait a few days longer and if I don't hear from him, shall "wake up" our new President and Senator "in future"[13] on the same subject.

My love to all at home—Mother and LuLu and accept much yourself from your most affectionate son.

Frank

CHAPTER VI

Triumph and Tragedy

THE DAWN OF 1865: like the coils of a giant anaconda, the blue-clad armies tightened their grip on the shrunken and battered Confederacy, crushing and suffocating. On January 15 Fort Fisher, guarding Wilmington, North Carolina, surrendered to an amphibious Union assault force. One of the Confederacy's last remaining bastions had fallen. Two weeks later, the Thirteenth Amendment to the U.S. Constitution abolishing slavery throughout the United States passed the House of Representatives by the requisite 2/3 majority (the Senate had approved it earlier) and was sent to the States for ratification. The exhausted man in the White House had placed the full power of his name and office behind this measure, earning the title "Great Emancipator."

The new year finds Frank Dickerson in receipt of orders posting him to Madison, Wisconsin. He looks forward to his new post with optimism.

Officers Hospital
Annapolis, Md.
January 10, 1865

Dear Father

I have not heard from home since my last writing, which seems a long time ago, yet I trust all is well there, in the full enjoyment of life's greatest blessing, health. At last I have received my orders for light duty, they came to hand this morning, of which the following is a copy. —

Special Orders   War Department
No. 10   Adjutant General's Office
                    Washington – Jan'y 7th 1865

x x x x x x x x x x x EXTRACT x x x x x x x x x x x

74. 1st Lieutenant F. W. Dickerson, 5th U.S. Cavalry, will report in person, without delay, to Lieutenant Colonel _____ Lowell, Chief Mustering and Disbursing Officer, at Madison, Wisconsin, for Mustering and Disbursing duty in the State of Wisconsin. xxxxxxxx
Per order of the Secretary of War official (signed) W.A. Nichols, Asst. Adjutant General

In compliance with the above order I intend leaving here for the West tomorrow. —
Madison, the capitol of the State is (as I learn from an officer who has been there) a beautiful city, the inhabitants hospitable, and the climate said to be favorable to my complaint "chronic Laryngitis."
Lieut. Col. Lowell the Chief Mustering Officer belongs to the 18th Infantry and is said to be a very fine man. —
I am very much pleased with the idea of a change giving me something to do — my health has not improved much since last writing — Direct your next letter to me as "Ass't Commissary of Musters" at Madison Wis. My love to Mother and Lulu and accept much yourself,
*   From your most affectionate son*
*   Frank*
Hon. J.G. Dickerson
Belfast, Me.

P.S. Please write often and send me some of the Maine papers.
*   F.W.D.*

Suddenly, en route to Wisconsin, Frank's optimism briefly turns to the lament of a young man who is close to collapse, but determined to forge ahead.

Sherman House
Chicago, January 15th, 1865

Dear Father

I arrived here yesterday afternoon after a long, tedious and wearisome ride by day and night from Baltimore, a distance of about 840 miles. I left Baltimore Thursday evening and arrived here Saturday afternoon. I was very much exhausted and worn out on my arrival here but a good night's rest here last night makes me feel a little better this morning. I was fearful yesterday that I should have to give way entirely and go to bed, but I have made up my mind that I'll not do that as long as I can walk. I am taking Cod Liver Oil now which I think relieves my cough somewhat. I hope the bracing atmosphere of Wisconsin may relieve me of it entirely. I intend to leave for Madison tomorrow. Will write from there after I get settled. —

My love to all at home.

Aff'y your son
Frank

Hon. J.G. Dickerson
Belfast

His next letter dated January 18, describes his duties and happily, a return of "a good deal of zest and spirit."

I arrived here Monday night about 12 o'clock and reported the following morning (yesterday), and today I have entered upon my duties. I have been assigned to the charge of the disbursing office where all disbursements and payments of monies for the "collecting organizing and

*drilling of Volunteers" for bounties and other purposes
are made for the State. I received $20,000.00 from the
officer I relieved and I expect to receive $100,000.00 from
Washington in a few days. — It is a big responsibility that
I trust and hope I can carry out the business honestly and
correctly. — Although I have a large safe in my office, yet I
deposit all my funds in the National Bank of this city which
is an acknowledged depository for government monies, and
make all my disbursements by checks on the bank. — The
officer that I relieved was Lieut. Col. Giddings 16th Infin.
[Infantry] (in the Register as Major G. R. Giddings 14th
Infin.) an old army officer who has had long experience in
such business, unfortunately he left here before I arrived. —
I have two offices on the lower floor of a large building (the
offices connected like those in the Custom House), one of
which is occupied by myself and chief clerk, the other by the
other clerks. I have 6 clerks including the chief, two of them
are citizens and 4 soldiers, detailed enlisted men. Col.
[Charles S.] Lovell's office is in the story above me, he has
two or three officers in his office with him and a number of
clerks. — the Col. is a Prv. [Provost] Mar. [Marshall] Gen'l of
the State of Supt. of Recruiting Service and Chief Must'g and
Disb'y Officer of the State. So far as I have seen of him, I
believe I shall like him very much.*

*I board at the Capitol House right across the road from
my office, it is a very good hotel about the size of the
American House though I am happy to say far superior to it
in all its appointments. — The legislature is in session here
and attracts many from all parts of the state. I haven't seen
much of the city yet or of its people, yet I am already
inclined to be prejudiced in its favor.*

*My health is much better than when I wrote from Chicago,
in fact, I entered upon my duties this morning with a good
deal of zest and spirit, the idea of something to do, and being
kept busy all day (after so long in idleness) was rather inspiring and I believe it will do me good. — My disbursements
for the day were several, being about $500 in small amt's. —*

MICHELE LEACH

The American House, on Belfast's Main Street, was originally known as the Eagle Hotel. It was built in 1824 and opened for business in 1825. (Courtesy Waldo County Register of Deeds)

Frank especially relished the "dry, clear and cold" weather, but confessed to homesickness in his January 27 letter.

> *Madison, Wis*
> *Jan'y 27th 1865*
>
> *Dear Father*
> *I am pleased to acknowledge the receipt of a long letter from you written before you knew of my arrival here, as well also as the receipt of several Maine papers one of which contained a very interesting account of the proceedings of the Supreme Judicial Court in session at Belfast. You cannot imagine what a great treat it is to me to receive letters and papers from the east. — Now that I*

*am so far away from home and friends I feel it more
than ever—in fact it appears to me now as if I was
isolated from all former friends and associations. It is
fearfully lonesome out here. I think I never experienced
such loneliness before—I think I wrote in a previous letter
that the people of this locality were inclined to be
hospitable to strangers. — If I did it was altogether
premature, it was a great mistake, made before I had any
opportunity of judging for myself. I do not wish to judge
them harshly on so short an acquaintance but will merely
say that present appearances do not indicate much
cordiality or regard for persons temporarily with them.
The same is the case with all the officers here, and were it
not for the fact that I am personally quite comfortably
located, I should be very much discontented. — I think
my health has improved somewhat, even in the short time
I have been here. The weather has been clear and cold, the
sleighing excellent. I stand the cold weather much better
than I expected after coming from a warmer climate. —
Business is quite dull with me now but I suppose it will
start up again next month when the new draft
commences. — I shall expect you to write often, and will
try to do the same. Also don't forget to send me papers. I
have no changes to record since my last writing in regard
to myself — I have not as yet received your letter
containing Mr. Hamlin's note which you say you
forwarded to me at Annapolis but I presume it will be
sent to me —*

*The military situation appears to be most favorable to
the Union Army. Fort Fisher is the last greatest triumph
and what a rebuke upon Butler and Weitzel's[1] former
attack and what a commentary of their military skill and
reputation as military men. — My hopes are centered in
Sherman and his army. My love to Mother and Lulu and
accept much yourself from your most affectionate son*
Frank

Having captured Savannah, General Sherman marched through the interior of South Carolina, heading for a rendezvous with Grant at Petersburg. Brushing aside weak Rebel resistance, the Union juggernaut captured Columbia, the State capitol, on February 17. That night, flames, fanned by gusty winds, swept the city. Sherman blamed fleeing Confederate arsonists, while Southerners ever since have blamed Sherman. No matter: Columbia was largely destroyed. "Hell was empty", a Southern minister snarled, "and all its devils were in this devoted city, learning new deviltry from Yankee teachers. A perfect reign of terror existed."[2] Meanwhile, Charleston, the very symbol of secession and Southern nationalism, abandoned by its defenders, surrendered to the bluecoats. And Sherman, after destroying Columbia's railroad stations, storehouses and other buildings useful to the Confederates, moved on inexorably.

Meanwhile, Frank talks wistfully about his diminished career and, with unconcealed disdain, about the quality of soldiers from Belfast.

Madison, Wis
Feb. 12th 1865

Dear Father

I am in receipt of two letters from you, one having been forwarded from Annapolis enclosing Mr. Hamlin's letter, the other of a recent date and from home. — I am deeply grateful to Mr. Hamlin for his kindness and I have no doubt that it was through his influence that I got away. The War Dept. is not sending any sick officers on light duty now, only those that are or have been wounded and not recovered. Of the Regular Officers that were at Annapolis sick, I was the only one that got away in light duty — and I attribute it to Mr. H. — I received a few days since, a letter from Mr. Merrill explaining his reasons for not answering my letter and offering his services etc. Since my last writing, I have had a partial change in the business of my office — Col. Giddings, my predecessor and who was ordered before the Retiring Board with a view of retirement, has returned, the Board having failed to retire him. Through his influence at Washington, he got ordered back here again. I am very glad of this, as he will—or rather already has—relieved me of the chief Disbursing duty, a responsibility I am glad to get off my shoulders. I shall continue to disburse, but my disbursements will be small to what they were. In addition to this duty I now do all the mustering out of service. Recruiting is going on very fast in this State. 4 new regt's have been raised under the President's last call for a draft, besides all that have gone into veterans organizations, nevertheless, there will have to be a draft in many localities. It looks to me as if Maine was behind hand on the coming draft. I am quite sure that Belfast will not fill her quota. It is a notorious fact (in my mind at least) that the young and able bodied men of that city have fearfully shirked the responsibility of this war, and even those who were patriotic enough to volunteer (and from whom much was naturally expected) seem with a few honorable exceptions, to have signally failed. Ansel White seems to be the only one of the young men of B[elfast] now in the service that has achieved any reputation or glory as a soldier. — His conduct in the field has, so far as I have been able to learn, from those associated with him, been ever worthy of a true soldier. I rejoice in his success. Belfast ought to be proud of having such an officer. He ought to have more rank. Where is the ambition of the young men of B? Can Belfast boast of having a single Colonel (men in or out of the field) in any of the Maine Regt's? I think not. For my part, I say (and not boastingly either) that all my ambition is centered in the hopes that I may so far recover my health again in the spring, not that I am at all dissatisfied with my present position for everything is as satisfactory as I could wish for as regards my duties here, but I feel that all the times I have been (unavoidably) absent from the field — I am losing a reputation which might otherwise have been gained. I want to get a Brevet,[3] it is the only thing we can get in the Regular Army to reward us. — I sometimes think I should have done better if I had gone into the Volunteer Army. I am confident that I should have had much more rank than I now have and in all probability much more reputation with the world. — At the same time I am very glad that I didn't, and never had regretted, the step that led me into the 5th Cav'ly. I am highly satisfied with my present position and at the time contented. I am happy in the thought of being able (even while out of health) to serve the government. Col. Giddings with whom I am associated is a very fine gentleman and treats me with great kindness. He is son of the celebrated "Josh" Giddings of Ohio.

My love to all at home, return a kiss from me to Lulu.

Affectionately your son
Frank

In his next letter, Frank reports that business is picking up.

Must'g 2 Dist'g Office
Madison, Wis
Feb 27th 1865

Dear Father

[I] have been so much occupied with my official duties during the past ten days that I have scarcely had time to do much letter writing. Business has taken a wonderful start with us lately, troops arriving here for "Muster In" and out of service, faster than we can, with our small force, take care of — Last week I mustered out the 3rd U.S. Cav'y, besides a great many men from different organizations whose time of service has expired, paid the U.S. bounties of a part of the 47th Wis., new organization which left for the field today, together with

the numerous other duties attendant upon an office like this. — Recruiting in the state goes on very rapidly. 4 new rgts. have already been raised under the President's last [call], and three more are in process of completion. — For the last month, the weather in this locality has been very mild. No sleighing of any consequence, and no snow storms of any consequence except a few sprinklings which would not make sleighing good more than a day.

My health remains about the same as at last writing, no material change that I can perceive for better or worse — I received this evening a letter from Cousin John Dickerson, informing me of his desire to come west and asking me if I could aid him in obtaining a situation as clerk or asst. clerk. I am glad to see such a desire on his part, to embark into something for himself and shall see what I can do for him. I am very sorry indeed that he did not write me sooner, as I could have given him a week ago a clerkship of $75 per month with a prospect of having it raised to $100. — We have been obliged to employ three new citizen clerks within the last two weeks on account of the increase of our business. Col. Giddings employed as his Chief Clerk Seth Cushman, a brother of James, at a salary of $125 per month. Seth resigned from the army about two months since and returned to Jamesville a city about 40 miles distant from here where he formerly resided. Col. Giddings and myself went down to see him about two weeks since, and he came up here last week and accepted the place. He will enter upon his duties on the 1st of March. — I am in hopes I may be able to get John a place in some of the offices here, before long, if possible a place in my office. — I shall however, offer him no inducements for him to come until I am quite certain of a place for him. The Legislators of the state [convened?] on the 2nd of March and fortunately I have been honored with an invitation, but probably shall not attend.

My love to all at home Mother and Lulu and accept
much yourself from your most affectionate son.
                    F. W. Dickerson

Early in February, President Lincoln and Secretary of State William H. Seward had met with Confederate Commissioners Vice President Alexander H. Stephens, former U.S. Supreme Court Justice John A. Campbell and former U.S. Senator and Confederate Secretary of State Robert M.T. Hunter aboard the *River Queen* in Hampton Roads, to discuss a possible peace. The conference foundered on Lincolns's insistence that rebelling Southern States acknowledge United States authority as a precondition to further negotiations. And so the war went on to its bitter conclusion.

Frank's letter of March 27 makes no mention of great events transpiring on the battle-front, confining itself to less cosmic matters.

What surprised me most of all in your letter was the
engagement of "Jessie" White to Dr. Flanders. I was not
aware that the Dr. went into society at all in B[elfast] and
this engagement causes me much wonderment and I cannot
understand how it was brought about. — On the other hand
I am not at all surprised to learn that Horace Noel is to be
married and only wonder that his union with some young
lady has not been consummated before. I believe he has
from time to time been in love with nearly all the young
ladies of his class in B[elfast]. I fear I shall have to look
somewhere else, besides in Belfast if engagements continue
to increase in that locality as fast as they have in a year or
two past. —

Our winter has almost disappeared, leaving scarcely a
vestige behind as a token of farewell, and we are now
having very fair Spring weather, it is mild and warm and
the frost is nearly out of the ground. — The Legislature is the
weather-cock for Spring in this latitude, as it never adjourns
until it is time for the farmers to put their wheat in. I find

*that the Spring weather does not agree with me quite as well
as the winter did, though I am quite well and suppose it will
not last long. — Recruiting lags a little now a days, and my
business has been very dull for the past ten days. It will
probably liven up again next month and the month
following as there are several regiments to be mustered out
during those months. I enclose you a photograph of Col.
Chas. S. Lovell 14th U.S. Infin. the Actg. Asst Pro. Mar Gen'l,
Superintendent of the Vol. Recruiting Service and Chief
Mustering and Disbursing Officer of the State of Wis. He is
one of the finest gentlemen I ever met, respected and loved
by everyone that knows him. — He has just been promoted
to the Colonelcy of the 14th Infy.*

Following the Battle of Five Forks (April 1), where Grant
crushed Lee's right flank, captured 4,500 Confederates and
threatened the crucial South Side Railroad, General Lee advised
President Jefferson Davis that Richmond must be abandoned to
salvage the Army of Northern Virginia. That Army, like a great
mortally wounded animal, dragged itself westward, dribbling
deserters like drops of blood. On April 2, the same day Richmond
fell, Frank must have rejoiced also over the great victory of
General James H. Wilson, cavalry commander extraordinaire,
who whipped the legendary Confederate cavalryman General
Nathan Bedford Forrest and captured Selma, Alabama, a vital
Confederate manufacturing center. Wilson's Selma campaign,
one of the greatest cavalry triumphs of the war, must have made
Lieutenant Dickerson regret even more than usual his non-
combatant exile in chilly Wisconsin.

Lee's gaunt soldiers subsisted on a handful of corn a day, and
starving horses gnawed each other's tails in desperation. The
Confederate commander hoped to find food to keep his army
alive to fight another day. Federal cavalry punched at the gray
ranks, and blue-coat cavalry and infantry piled into the Army of
Northern Virginia at Sayler's Creek (April 6), capturing some
8,000 Rebels, as well as Lt. Gen. Richard S. ("Old Baldy") Ewell,
wooden leg and all! This last fight with the Army of the Potomac

spelled the end for Lee's emaciated Army. Two days later, faced with surrendering or fighting to the death, General Lee requested a meeting with General Grant. The latter, at the time, was suffering a migraine headache. It was cured instantly.

Poor Wilmer McLean! The owner of a home near Manassas Junction, he had been engulfed by the first battle of Bull Run, his barn turned into a field hospital, a shell smashing into his house. He vowed to take his family out of the war for good. So he moved to the peaceful village of Appomattox Court House, Virginia. Now, on April 9, 1865, the war caught up with the unfortunate Mr. McLean. The surrender ceremony took place in the parlor of his brick house. White-bearded General Lee, splendid in a new uniform, with a sash around his waist and a handsome sword at his side, looked more like the victor than the vanquished. Many Union officers, Generals Sheridan and Custer among them, peered curiously at the legendary Confederate. Then General Grant walked in. He had lost his baggage wagon temporarily and with it his dress uniform and sword. So he appeared in his working clothes, a private's blouse with the three stars of his rank stitched to gold-edged shoulder straps. One of his own staff sniffed, "Grant, covered with mud, in an old faded uniform, looked like a fly on a shoulder of beef."[4]

The two men exchanged pleasantries, then turned to surrender terms, agreeing that officers and men of the Army of Northern Virginia would promise not to fight again until properly exchanged. They could go home and resume their normal lives undisturbed by federal authorities. Officers could retain their side arms (Lee would not have to surrender his beautiful sword after all), all other weapons and army property to be handed over to the Army of the Potomac. And Confederate soldiers who owned their own mounts could take them home for spring planting. Grant also promised rations for the surrendered troops.

After meeting Grant's officers, General Lee left the house and drew on his gauntlets, striking one hand into the other as he stood lost in thought. Then he called for his horse "Traveller," sighed deeply as he swung into the saddle, and rode off to break the sad news to his men. A terrible scene followed this impressive one. Like greedy children scrambling for candy, Union officers looted McLean's house for souvenirs, shoving greenbacks at the outraged owner. Union Generals Sheridan and E. O. C. Ord secured the prize mementoes: the two tables used in the surrender room, one of which rode off on General Custer's shoulder, a gift from Sheridan to Libby Custer, the General's wife.

Later, Union Maj. Gen. Joshua L. Chamberlain, erstwhile Bowdoin College theology professor, supervised the moving ceremony at which the Rebels, many of them in tears, stacked their arms and battle flags before their conquerors.

On April 18, the remnants of the Army of Tennessee, once again commanded by General Joseph E. Johnston, surrendered to General Sherman in North Carolina, and in May, Confederate troops in the Department of Alabama, Mississippi and East Louisiana, and west of the great river, laid down their arms.

The Civil War was over.

Madison, Wis
April 10, 1865

Dear Father

I congratulate you on the recent successes of the Union Armies as manifested in the fall of Richmond and the surrender of the rebel army of "Northern Virginia." —
On receipt of the news of the fall of Richmond, the people of the city became wild with joy and excitement, stores and offices were closed all business suspended, salutes [fired], bands playing at the head of impromptu processions, speeches made and illuminations and whiskey wound up the evening entertainments. — It seemed almost impossible for many to throw off the excessive exuberance of their joy. — We received the news of the surrender of the "Army of Northern Virginia" about ten o'clock last night, a midnight salute was fired, bonfires illuminated the streets, and the noise of cheering resounded from all parts of the city, the whole city was alive with excitement in ½ an hour after the receipt of

the news. Today we are comfortably quiet. I consider the terms of surrender proposed by Grant as magnanimous in the extreme and very respectable for Lee to accept. — Praise God that war is virtually ended!! —

Since I wrote you last I have been up to Detroit Michigan — by order of Col. Lovell, for the purpose of cashing a govt draft, and brought the "Green backs" safely back. It was all in small bills and made a large package filling a large Carpet Bag. — I have not heard from home for some time, trust all are well. John gets along quite well and joins with me in sending love to all—

> *Affcy' Your Son*
> *Frank*

As Spring, 1865, approached, President Lincoln felt utterly exhausted, so worn out by the cruel pressures of war that he spoke of a tired spot within beyond the reach of healing rest. But April changed everything. Like Madison, Washington went mad with joy when Richmond fell and Lee surrendered. And in the White House, the weight of the world slipped from Lincoln's shoulders. His gaunt face glowed with a quiet joy and triumph beautifully captured in his last photographs. Now he could serve out his term, bringing healing and reconciliation to the torn Union, and then take a long-anticipated trip abroad with Mary before returning to Springfield and resuming his law practice.

Good Friday dawned balmy and blossomy. Lincoln met his Cabinet in excellent spirits, spoke of forgiveness for the former enemy and a Union firmly restored.

That misty evening, the Presidential carriage rolled through the White House gates, carrying the Lincolns to Ford's Theater and a performance of Tom Taylor's farce, "Our American Cousin." An exultant crowd, many men in Union blue, thronged the gas-lit theater as the Presidential party (including Major Henry R. Rathbone and Miss Clara Harris)[5] entered the spacious State Box to the strains of "Hail to the Chief." President and Mrs. Lincoln bowed to the wildly cheering audience, then took their seats, Lincoln sinking wearily into a large, overstuffed rocker. The play went on, and he thoroughly enjoyed the evening.

Shortly after ten, an intruder crept into the box. Had Lincoln turned, he would have recognized him instantly. Every American theatergoer knew the actor John Wilkes Booth. The youngest of a great theatrical family, Wilkes Booth specialized in roles calling for swordplay, gymnastic feats and the like. Spoiled, self-indulgent, a bit unstable, and a thoroughgoing gloryseeker, Booth dazzled audiences North and South before the war. He professed to love the Confederacy and despise the Union, but, significantly, never donned Confederate gray to fight for the Southern cause. While less exalted young men bled and died for their beliefs, Wilkes Booth merely trumpeted his, while earning a salary of some $20,000 a year. He despised with a great passion the President of the United States and even concocted a bizarre plot to kidnap Lincoln and whisk him away to Richmond, the ransom being the resumption of the prisoner exchange system suspended by General Grant. With the ending of the war, Booth resolved to murder his unbeatable enemy. Doubtless he hoped to plunge the Union into chaos, especially since his conspiracy called for the deaths of Secretary of State Seward and Vice President Johnson as well. But more important, he wanted to immortalize the name of John Wilkes Booth. And so the famous young actor with the ivory pallor, coat-black hair and drooping mustache, wearing riding clothes and spurred boots, stealthily approached Abraham Lincoln, holding a heavy-caliber, single shot derringer pistol in one hand and a wicked-looking dagger in the other.

Snuggled close to the President, Mary Lincoln murmured, "What will Miss Harris think of my hanging on to you so?" "She won't think anything about it," Lincoln replied.[6] His mind had framed its last thought. Booth fired at deadly range, the massive slug hitting the President behind the left ear, plowing through his brain, and lodging behind his right eye. Lincoln's left arm flew up convulsively. Then he slumped forward, his wife struggling to hold him in the chair.

The assassination, on Good Friday of 1865, of President Abraham Lincoln by John Wilkes Booth, at the time 26 years of age. With the President and his wife, Mary (seated beside him) was Clara Harris, daughter of Sen. Ira Harris of New York, and her fiance, Maj. Henry Rathbone. The single, massive slug from Booth's derringer hit the President behind his right ear. He died at 7:22 a.m. the next morning. (Library of Congress)

In the audience, a young Maine woman, Sarah Jane Hamlin Batchelder, sat with her new husband, Major George Batchelder, her brother General Charles Hamlin and his wife Sarah. This only daughter of former Vice President Hamlin had seen no flash:

> so although the direction was nearly known, everything was done so quickly the audience was completely paralyzed [*sic*] and presence of mind was wanting everywhere, what aroused all was the murderer crying out as he fairly reached the stage (having jumped from the box), "Sic Semper Tyrannis" and then something about the South which was not clearly heared [*sic*] by anyone but was in substance . . . Thus have I saved the South—

Major Batchelder turned to his wife and said "it is a man who boards at the National was there when we were there and who *looks just like Wilkes Booth.*"[7]

After a long night of hopeless struggle, Lincoln died at 7:22 a.m. the next morning, as rain began to fall and the smell of fresh earth mingled with the overpowering lilac scent floating through the deathroom window.

Frank Dickerson pens his most fascinating letter the day after the President's death.

Madison, Wis.
April 16th, 1865

Dear Father
You have doubtless 'ere this heard of the horrible assassination of our late beloved President Abraham Lincoln and of the attempted murder of our able Secretary of State, Mr. Seward. History furnished no parallel for the atrocity of these deeds. President Lincoln was stricken down while in the height of glory, popularity and personal happiness, his work was nearly completed, would to God he had been able to finish it and been spared to complete his remaining days in quiet and peace. — Enjoying the love and respect of the American

people, but an all wise Providence ruled otherwise, how true the lines "In the midst of life we are in death." The country was not prepared for the suddenness of this shock, to lose our President, as a time when rays of peace were commencing to dawn upon us and the prospects of happily settling our national difficulties was so apparent, I fear is an irreparable loss to the country, and in the event of Mr. Seward's death, who can fill his place? I know of no one, but we must hope for the best. This country is passing through an awful ordeal, yet my faith that it will come out triumphantly in the end is still unshaken. Let the people cast aside all personal prejudices they may have against Andrew Johnson and give to him and the armies of the United States their heartiest support, and we will soon wind up this rebellion and show to the world that the destinies of this country are not bound up in the life of one man (even though he may be head of the land) and that his death cannot paralyze the arm of the government or arrest the progress of its attempts to maintain its organization. President Johnson has always proved himself to be the right man for "emergencies" [even] if he did get drunk on his Inauguration Day (which I regard more of an accident than anything else), for which, considering all circumstances, a great allowance ought to be made, and I have faith that he will be fully equal to the trust and responsibility now imposed on him. [8]

I regret to say, that with the murderer of President Lincoln I had a slight acquaintance. He boarded at the same house in Baltimore ("Barnums") that I did when I was there last fall under medical treatment. I used to see him nearly every day, and was rather prepossessed than otherwise with his appearance. He was very intelligent, well educated and informed, possessing a fine looking exterior, to which he added a polite and courteous demeanor, which attracted people toward him and gained him much personal popularity. I should judge

A photograph of the first page of Frank Dickerson's "Lincoln Letter" of April 16, 1865, written the day after the President's death. The page, a vellum, measures 7¾ inches wide and 9¾ inches long. The engraving barely visible in the upper left corner includes the word Congress, *a likeness of the Capitol in Washington, and the initials A.P.CO., which probably stand for Army of the Potomac Command. (Collection of Lucy Richardson)*

*him to be about 30 years of age not over that. I have
conversed with him frequently both before and after [the]
presidential election, and though I knew him to be an
opponent of the administration, I never knew him to
express any very decided sentiments of partiality towards
any party or to utter one breath of disloyalty against
the government. He might have been deterred from
expressing himself fully to me on account of my being
an officer (towards whom people in Baltimore are very
careful what they say), for fear I would have him
arrested. In my slight acquaintance with him, I never
considered him a politician at all, or even particularly
interested in national affairs. He was engaged when I
knew him in "Oil Speculations" in Pennsylvania and
was reported to have been very successful, making quite
a fortune.[9] He is the last man I should ever think of to
commit such a deed, his very looks would belie the
fact, — And I yet can scarcely realize that it is the same
man. He associated with some of the strongest union men
in the city of Baltimore. What motives could actuate him
to the committal of such an atrocious and fiendish cause
I cannot divine or imagine. — Justice is in his track and
will follow him to the gallows. —*

Love to Mother and Lulu—

Aff'y Your Son
"Frank"

151

———◆———

Chapter VII

"Ave Atque Vale"

ON APRIL 10, 1865, Mayor Nehemiah Abbott of Belfast proclaimed:

> FELLOW CITIZENS OF BELFAST It is fitting that we should exchange congratulations over the fall of *Richmond*, the surrender of *General Lee* and his *army* and the *downfall* of the *Rebellion*. To that end, I respectfully request that all stores and places of business be closed at one of the clock this afternoon; that at the hour a salute of one hundred guns be fired; that at eight in the evening all private and public buildings and places of business be illuminated; and that at eight and a half the citizens generally, ladies and gentlemen, assemble at Peirce's Hall, where speeches, music, and dancing may be expected.[1]

And so Belfast rejoiced. An old wooden former law office was dragged to Custom House Square, crammed with flammable material, and torched for a glorious bonfire. Citizens thronged the streets, the uproar of celebration lasting until midnight.

Five days later, news of President Lincoln's murder plunged Belfast into mourning, with flags at half staff, buildings sheathed in crepe, minute guns booming, business suspended at the time of the funeral on April 19, and the city's preachers crying out for vengeance against the Confederate leadership. Reverend Wooster Parker of the First Congregational Church thundered that the Rebel leaders should be executed:

> If the doctrine is true, that men cannot forfeit their title to future salvation by any crimes they may commit, and if, upon departing this life, they enter upon a happier and more blissful one, and this is to be the lot of those whose guilt and criminality

no language can adequately describe, they should be sent swinging to glory![2]

In a letter to his stepmother on April 23, Frank tells of Madison's civic tribute to the martyred President.

We had arranged to have a grand military and civic funeral here the day that the same was had in Washington, great preparations were made, a magnificent funeral car was constructed, stands built for speakers in the Capitol Park etc., but the day, unfortunately was so stormy, that the funeral cortege was postponed, and the state house was thrown open to the public, at which place the other exercises occurred.

Frank notes optimistically, "My health appears to improve as Spring comes along, and I am in hopes it will become fully restored in a few months, so that I shall be able to make my annual visit home this year in good health."

My business has been very dull for the past month in fact almost nothing to do, which has inclined to make me feel somewhat discontented. However it being a good hunting season! and Col. Giddings an ardent lover of the sport! he and I have greatly enjoyed many leisure hours in the duck and pigeon shooting and sometimes our efforts have been very successful. —

Since the suspension of drafting and recruiting, we have been obliged to discharge several of our clerks, and expect soon to have to discharge men, I am in hopes though, to be able to retain John [Frank's cousin] at least as long as I remain here. He is a very good boy and tries hard to do his work well. I am quite well satisfied with him and like him very much. Col. Giddings also likes him. We have hardly recovered from the shock of President Lincoln's death. I never knew such general public scorn [presumably toward the assassin] as has gone among the people of this state. All of the stores, offices, and private houses still continue to be draped in mourning and nearly every citizen and soldier wears some appropriate badge of mourning to mark their respect and love for the deceased.

Lieut. Ellsworth of the 11th United States Infantry who has been on duty here for some time as Asst. Supt. of Recruiting Service, was last week ordered to his Reg't, "Othello's occupation being gone" — It is impossible for me to calculate upon the length of time I shall remain here, it is probable I may be relieved at any time now, although if peace is soon achieved, and the Regt's are not mustered out in the field, it is more than likely for me to remain some time longer. If the Regt's should be mustered out in the field, by "Commisary's of Musters" before returning to their respective States, then my occupation will be gone, I shall be ordered to my reg't—

I am anxious to hear from father, have not heard from him since the death of President Lincoln, I trust he does not yet despair of the Republic, and hope he has confidence in our new President Andrew Johnson. He was formerly a great admirer of him. — John joins me in sending love to all. —

Affectionately
Frank

In his next letter, Frank speaks of the new President.

Madison, Wis
May 7th 1865

Dear Father

Yours of a recent date was duly received, and its contents afforded me much pleasure. I was above all glad to see that you had so much confidence in our new President. I think he has commenced right and in such a manner as to secure him the confidence of all loyal men. I am anxiously awaiting to see his proclamation which shall officially proclaim his views and the policy by which his administration will be guided. In some particulars it has already been foreshadowed in his recent public

*speeches and official acts. — His views regarding the
final disposition of leading rebels and trait[or]s meets
with my hearty approbation and I have no doubt the
country will endorse and sustain them. I do not go in
for a wholesale slaughter of public men in the south
who have taken a prominent part in the support and
maintenance of the rebellion, but believe that such men
as [Jefferson] Davis, [John C.] Breckinridge and a few
others should be brought to justice and punished
according to the extremity of their offenses. — Jeff Davis
is still at large, a fugitive from justice with a price set
upon his head, but he cannot long escape the vengeance
of his own people and I should not be surprised at any
time to hear that he has been captured or assassinated by
them, and finally, if all the efforts fail, he will be hunted
down by our armies like a wild beast and meet the fate
usually accorded to them. — I have had sad news from
my regiment since last writing: during the close of the
fighting in front of Richmond Capt. Drummond was
instantly killed. Capt. Leib seriously wounded. Lieut
Denney wounded and taken prisoner — Capt. Drummond
was a splendid gentleman and faithful and efficient
officer. [B]oth personally and officially he will be a great
loss to us and one not easily replaced. Capt. Leib is at his
home and doing finely, he writes in the best of spirits and
thinks he will speedily recover. — The regiment has
suffered severely during the past few months and only has
two officers with it, the Adjutant and Lieut Urban who
has twice been wounded. Capt. Mason with his squadron
still remains at the head Qur's of the Army — I hope there
will be no more fighting for some time and the regt. may
have a chance to go to some peaceful locality to refit,
recruit, and rest [a]while after their long and arduous
labors in the field. The Reg't ought all to be consolidated
and stationed at one place with a good complement of
officers: there are no Second Lieutenants in it, and these
vacancies ought to be at once filled. — My company has*

been commanded by my First Serg't ever since I left it, 6 months ago.

The Weather has been delightful during the present month and I can almost feel my health improving every day. I am and have been busy for some time past Mustering troops out of service under the recent orders of the War Dept, reducing the military establishment with this business. John is well and gives general satisfaction in the office, he sends his love to all at home. I hope to be able to make you a visit some time during the summer or fall in good health so I can enjoy myself. —

I have no objections to remaining here all summer now that the war is virtually over for I think it must be a delightful place in summer time.

Write soon and often. Love to Mother and Lulu. Affectionately

> *Your son*
> *Frank*

Frank could scarcely have been pleased by President Andrew Johnson's Reconstruction policy, as outlined in his May proclamation. As military Governor during the war, the grim and indomitable Tennessean had breathed fire and brimstone against the Rebellion and had spoken darkly of gallows festooned with leading Confederates! But power and responsibility tempered his views, and he promised amnesty to Confederates taking a simple oath of allegiance to the U.S. Several classes of leading Rebels were excepted from general amnesty to be sure, but the President granted special pardons generously, virtually upon request.

Johnson viewed reunion as a healing process, to be carried out quietly and with non-draconian requirements for former Confederate States to be restored to their normal relationship to the Union. He appointed a provisional governor for each of the seven unrestored Confederate States and charged that official to call a convention elected by "loyal" citizens (Presidentially-pardoned Confederates included). Such a convention must repudiate secession, abolish slavery, and disown the State war debt. The State's new legislature must ratify the Thirteenth Amendment. Admission to Congress of the State's Senators and Representatives would complete restoration.

Every Confederate State but Texas had complied with the terms of Johnson's restoration plan by December, 1865, allowing the President to announce proudly in his first State of the Union message that the Union was once again made whole. The stage was set for a titanic struggle between President and Congress for the soul of Reconstruction.

Earlier historians cast Andrew Johnson in the role of a gallant Presidential David defending Southern rights from a bestial Goliath of a Radical-dominated Congress bent upon brutally punishing and prostrating the former Confederate States. Current historical thinking sees Johnson as a woefully stubborn political outsider and loner, ignoring and flouting legitimate Northern public opinion in the name of a narrow, crabbed constitutionalism. That public opinion demanded evidence of Southern repentance, guarantees that the rebellion would not be rekindled and, above all, protection for the freed slaves.[3] Certainly Frank Dickerson would have endorsed the latter views. But he never lived to see the triumph of Congressional Reconstruction (which dismantled Johnsonian "restoration"), the ultimate impeachment of the President in 1868 and his acquittal in the U.S. Senate by a single vote.

But all this strife over Reconstruction lay in the future as the victorious soldiers paraded before President Johnson in the Grand Review of the Armies of the Union. From all over the South, troops streamed into Washington—150,000 strong. By night, their campfires, blazing on the surrounding hills, wreathed the capitol city in light; by day, rubber-necking country boys explored the city, gawking at the Capitol, the White House, and the unfinished Washington Monument and tasting the forbidden delights of Washington's numerous saloons and brothels.

After a spell of intermittent rain, the sun shone brightly for the Grand Review. Cavalry clattered into the city on May 22 and encamped near the Capitol, which had a large gilded eagle over the front door and a banner on the north end proclaiming, "The only national debt we can never pay is the debt we owe to the victorious Union soldiers."[4]

The Army of the Potomac followed, and Capitol Square rang with bugle calls, singing, and goodnatured hellraising. The parade began next day, thousands of Cavalrymen preceding the magnificent but hardluck Army of the Potomac infantry, which marched down Pennsylvania Avenue, 20 abreast, to beating drums, ringing bugles, and the clamor of massed military bands. Twenty-five hundred District of Columbia children lined the parade route, girls in white dresses, boys sporting white trousers and blue jackets. Bouquets and wreaths showered the horsemen and marching men, a blizzard of blossoms hitting George Armstrong Custer, whose horse bolted in terror, causing the General to temporarily lose his hat and saber.

Only soldiers who had actually seen battle could march, but it took six hours for the cavalry, infantry, and artillery to pass the reviewing stand outside the White House. Splashes of color enlivened the endless streams of blue: the red diamond insignia of the kepis of Phil Kearney's sadly-diminished command; the crossed red swords of the cavalry; the green sprigs of boxwood stuck in the caps of the jaunty Irish Brigade; the hundreds of regimental and American flags snapping in the breeze, and adorning the front of the new Treasury building, the famous hand-painted Treasury Guards flag which had snared Booth's spur.*

General Sherman's armies marched next day. Lean, sun-burned men, wearing sugar-loaf hats and loose-fitting blouses, they looked bigger and less neat than their Eastern comrades, but they moved with equal precision. Sherman's "bummers", those tireless foragees who had plucked Georgia clean of foodstuffs on the great march from Atlanta to the sea, strode proudly along amidst their

> pack mules loaded with turkeys, geese, children, and bacon, and here and there a chicken-coop strapped on the saddle with a cackling brood peering out through the slats. Then came

cows, goats, sheep, donkeys, crowing roosters, and in one instance a chattering monkey. Mixed in with these was a procession of fugitive blacks—old men, stalwart women, and grinning pickaninnies of all sizes, and ranging in color from a raven's wing to a new saddle. This portion of the column called forth shouts of laughter and continuous rounds of applause.

Thus, General Horace Porter, Grant's erstwhile aide-de-camp, described the bizarre scene.[5]

Another general wrote sadly of the cruelly-shrunken regiments in both Eastern and Western armies:

Had the eye of the spirit been opened . . . the spectator would have seen by the side of each man, who moved firmly and proudly in the victorious column, three wounded and crippled men, limping and stumbling in their eager desire to keep up with their more fortunate comrades [*sic*], while with the four stalked one pale ghost.[6]

In his next letter, Frank writes of 5th U.S. Cavalry comrades whose ghostly presence might have been felt at the Grand Review. But there was joyous new life, too.

May 25th 1865
Mustering and Disbursing Office
Madison, Wis.

Dear Father
Yours of the 16th was duly received, its contents
affording me the greatest pleasure. — I congratulate
you and Mother on the recent happy event which has
increased our little household and which is destined to
become a source of the greatest happiness to you both. —
I hail with joy this happy event as a most auspicious and
favorable omen, — a "consummation fervently to be
wished" — I greet with many true and earnest wishes (of
health, prosperity, and happiness through life) the little
one's dawn upon earth. May he live to a "ripe old age",

the pride and joy of his parents, the friend and delight of his brother and sisters. My pleasure on receiving the news was only increased by my great surprise, — I have long secretly wished for the consummation of such an event, and at last all my hopes are anticipated. I can but again report my hearty congratulations. I trust that Mother may soon regain her usual good health and that "baby" may flourish under her maternal care. — I am overwhelmed with business at present. (Mustering out) working day and evening. Am doing all I can to help a reduction of the national expenses, am mustering out men faster than they can be paid, am as anxious to get them out of service as they are themselves and much more so than a good many of their officers are. —

My regiment I believe is in Washington. It had the honor of escorting Major Gen'l Merritt Comd'g the Cavalry of the Army of the Potomac (in Sheridan's absence) at the recent grand review in W[ashington]. It has suffered severely during the last campaign. Capt. Drummond having been killed. Capt. Leib seriously wounded, and Lieut Denney, wounded and captured, the loss in enlisted men was also large. This is a heavy loss considering there was [sic] only six officers with it during the whole time. Thus, all men, only three officers with it, Lieut's Hastings and Harris. — My health is quite good— My love to friends in Bangor and to Mother, Lulu and "Aabel"⁷ when you go home. John sends love to all—

Affectionately your son.
Frank

Hon. J.G. Dickerson

Frank's love for his step-mother can be seen clearly in his May 28 letter.

I have received your several letters of recent dates informing me first of the critical situation of Mother's health and finally of the good prospects of her recovery.

*Your first letter filled me with many gloomy forebodings
and caused the greatest anxiety while your last caused the
greatest joy and hope — I trust that by this time she may be
past all danger, though I am still quite anxious about her,
as I received no letter from you last evening. — God grant
she is now convalescent and doing well . . . Do not fail to
keep me advised often of Mother's situation. Nothing new
here. Lieut. Purcell 1st Inf'y, formerly Mustering Officer here,
has been relieved and sent to his Regiment, which throws all
the Mustering business in the state on my hands.*

Business presses heavily upon Frank, in such a way as to
"slightly impair my health, although I have not been so [sickly]
but what I could be about all the time."

*Col. Lovell, seeing I was not quite as well as usual, told
me to go off for 5 or 6 days and rusticate, that Col.
Giddings would attend to my business for me during my
absence. I told him I didn't think it was right for me to go
away when there was so much to do, and that if he would
relieve me from part of my duties, I thought I could get
along all right. He has done so and Col. Giddings is now
doing part of the Mustering out and I am getting up again
as usual.*

Still, he finds himself writing 400 signatures a day, "besides
attending to a hundred other duties of different natures."

He hopes to visit Belfast in the summer.[8] Meanwhile, he takes a
few days off.

*My health has improved somewhat since last writing.
I went down to Milwaukee during 4th of July week,
remaining over the 4th, having a respite of 3 or 4 days from
my labors in the office. The Wisconsin Soldiers Home Fair
was in full blast at the time and was a great success,
realizing over $100,000. for the establishment of a Home
for disabled soldiers. I wonder the State of Maine don't
originate something of the kind. . . .*
My regiment is very delightfully situated up in the

161

*mountains of Maryland at a place called Cumberland.
I hope it may stay there during the winter. — I hope to get
away from here by 1st of October and join it, as it will be
impossible for me to stand another winter in this climate.
For the last 3 or 4 days we have had to have a fire at our
hotel to keep ourselves comfortable. The season has been a
cold and rainy one and very unpropitious for invalids so
far. The crops however are looking finely and bid fair to
yield rich harvest.*

*I hope it may be possible for me to visit home during the
fall but don't see much prospect of it now, shall come if I
can.*[9]

Back on the job, things ease a bit, and Frank plans to rejoin his
regiment.

*We are as usual hard at work Mustering out the Vol.
forces to which there seems to be no end. We employ in our
office 14 citizen clerks and 2 enlisted men, all of whom are
kept constantly at work. Co'l Giddings has taken the work of
Mustering out of my hands for the past weeks, and my duties
have been comparatively light to what they were. I have
been engaged in the meantime in examining the accounts
of Mustering Out officers and going through certificates on
non-indebtedness so that they could obtain a final
settlement with the gov't and draw their pay. This duty at
first was rather arduous, I had so many to examine, but it is
rapidly decreasing, and for the past week, I have had but
little to do. I have had opportunities for being out of doors
more and I find that it has done me a good deal of good
and I feel much better for this little season of rest. —*

*I fear we shall lose Col. Lovell, our present able and
beloved Ch'f Must'g Officer, as he received an order from the
War Dept the other day, saying that all the officers of the
14th U.S. Inf'y (of which he is Col.) on detached duty, would
be immediately relieved and ordered to report to Hart's
Island, N.Y. The reg't will probably embark from there to
California. I have received three or four private letters from*

the officers of my reg't asking me to come back to them,
saying that they are located in a beautiful place at
Cumberland, M'd. a remarkable healthy locality as is
proven from the fact that there is not a sick man in the reg't.
Capt Leib, my old friend, is in command and writes me that
he is building a neat cottage in which [I] shall have a room
if I will come on. I shall probably remain here until Sept'r
when, if not relieved, I shall make application to re-join the
reg't. — Capt Mason still commands the escort of the Lieut.
Gen'l, and is located in Washington, but I prefer to join the
reg't rather than remain about W[ashington]. The weather
here this summer has been unusually severe for my troubles,
cold, damp and rainy. For the past six weeks I don't think
we have had two days of continuous dry weather. We have
had no warm weather since the last of May and first of June,
not one day in which it was warm enough to wear a linen
coat and be comfortable. We must have dry weather soon or
the crops will be ruined. If the coming month is not more
genial than the last have been, I shall take the first
opportunity of returning South. How is Mother and the
baby? I trust by this time she has nearly recovered her usual
good health. [10]

But Frank is still needed in Madison, now more than ever.

We have had some important changes in our office since
my last letter. Col. Lovell has been relieved by Lt. Col.
Giddings and I have relieved Col. G[iddings] as Disbursing
Officer, which duties I will have to perform in connection
with Mustering Out until some officer relieves me from the
latter. Col. G. has already moved out of the office, turned
over to me all the gov't funds and property and put me in
chief charge and Disbursing duty of the State. . . . The
Mustering business is gradually decreasing, so that my
duties will not be increased much after all by this change. . . .
It is impossible for me to think of coming home while on
duty here. I hope to be relieved from here in October. — I
shall make application to be at that time and when relieved

*shall also apply for a 30 days "Leave" previous to joining
my reg't.*

*I was rather surprised at what you wrote about Ellen, but
if the young man is all that you have reason to suppose he
is, I must say that I am very gratified indeed.*

*Ellen is too young by two years to be married, (but I
suppose she is willing to wait and the young man ought
to be also) but I consider that an engagement with a
respectable and honorable young man for that time would
be of great advantage to her. — I hope to hear from you
again after you have made up your mind on the subject. —
John joins with me in sending love to all. —*

*As for myself I never shall think of getting married until I
have something besides a Lieut's pay to support myself and
Madam _____ — and that is a long way off.*[11]

Frank expresses concern at news of his father's illness and
urges reassurance from home.

*I am as well as usual, with but little to do. Our business is
decreasing so fast, that I think the prospects of my getting
away next month are very good. . . . I think I shall have no
trouble in getting back to my regt whenever I get ready to
make the application.*[12]

"I was rejoiced to hear that your illness was not more serious
than you represent and that your recovery was so speedy," Frank
writes Judge Dickerson on September 21. "I think we all have
reason to be grateful to divine Providence for such a result. God
grant that you may not be so affected again in a long long time."
Politics enliven the Wisconsin scene:

*I think my health is better now that it has been at any
previous time during the last year, which I believe is partly
due to the relaxation of my official duties as well as to the
genial influences of the summer climate in this locality. —
We have had two political state conventions here during the
past two weeks, both Republican and Democratic, neither of
which endorsed the negro suffrage doctrine. There is a split*

in the Republican ranks on that question and those in favor of that doctrine are to hold another convention at Janesville next to pass resolutions endorsing that doctrine. They will not, however, bolt the ticket nominated here but will vote it while ignoring the platform on which their candidates stand. — The military are conspicuous on both the Democratic and Republican tickets, two Generals leading each ticket. I think it well enough for Maine to show her gratitude to the soldiers in some such manner. Gen'l Fairchilds [sic], Repub'n candidate for Governor, lost an arm in the service, as well also as did Gen'l Montgomery the Democratic candidate for Atty Gen'l. Gen'l Tom Allen, Repub. candidate for Sec'y of State, has also been wounded 3 or 4 times. I have yet to hear of any returned soldier in the State of Maine having received any such evidence of the peoples gratitude. The military men selected for the nominations above referred to are men of eminent ability and well worthy to be supported by the people. —

Frank's next letter combines alarm at continuing news of Judge Dickerson's illness with a sprightly account of General William Tecumseh Sherman's visit to the Wisconsin capitol. This, the longest of Frank's letters, recounts meeting the General and hearing his views on Reconstruction.

October 1, 1865

Dear Father
. . . John [Dickerson] had a letter from his father the other day in which he stated you have been sick for 4 weeks, and as I haven't heard from you for some time, I am fearful that you haven't yet recovered your health (though you wrote so encouragingly in your last [letter]) or that you may have had a relapse. — Please let me know immediately on receipt of this just how you are, — concealing nothing — that my anxiety may be relieved. Do not hesitate to telegraph me if at any time your

*sickness should approach anything like seriousness, and
I will come home, no matter what stands in the way.
I trust in God that my apprehensions are groundless
and that you are again in possession of His greatest
blessing. — God grant that you may be spared to us
many years longer and that a bright career of usefulness
may be yours in the future. — My dear father I am most
anxious about you, perhaps unnecessarily so, but Uncle
Kendrick's [Dickerson] letter, has filled me with many
apprehensions; he also said that I had better come home;
surely I should not hesitate a moment to do so if I thought
you were really ill. — I wait patiently to hear from you
or from other at home. —*

*My health is better now that at any time in a year past.
I thank you Heavenly Father that it is so, and pray that it
may continue to improve —*

*It is so much improved that I have left the hotel where I
have been boarding ever since I came here — solely on
that acc't — and have taken a private boarding house. I
am much pleased with the change, it seems so much more
like home. If ever one was totally disgusted with hotel
living I am, nothing but indisposition could have kept me
there as long as it did — I now rejoice in some of the
comforts and sociability of a home.*

*The great sensation here for the past two days has been
the arrival of Gen'l Sherman — The Gen'l arrived from
Janesville where he had been in attendance in the State
Fair yesterday afternoon at 4 o'clock, and was escorted
from the depot by all the military at this post, and by the
State and city officers of the army on duty here and
citizens in carriages, making a long procession. Your
humble servant rode in the second carriage in rear of the
Genl's and was introduced to him and had a hearty shake
of the old hero's hand. — He looks finely, so those say
who have seen him before. On the arrival at the Park he
received a Major Genl's salute, and was welcomed by the
Mayor of the city; he responded in a very neat and*

166

appropriate speech, which won the respect of all. He is a good speaker. Naturally so, talks with ease, and readiness and showed no signs of embarrassment at any time during the formalities of his reception. He charmed everybody by the grace of his manners. He is the most affable, easy, and courteous gentleman that I have ever met in the army. In his personal appearance, he is remarkable, looks every inch a soldier and gentleman and could not but remind even a stranger that he was a remarkable man. — He is, as Judge [James R.] Doolittle remarked in his speech last night, "the very personification of the eagle of victory" — He is the guest of Gen'l Fairchilds (the Union candidate for Governor this fall) during his stay here. He leaves tonight for Milwaukee.

Last night the Gen'l was escorted to the Assembly Chamber where he made a few brief remarks and was followed by Senator Doolittle in a two hours speech, which was one of the most powerful efforts I ever listened to. It was the occasion of a grand Union Rally and Judge D[oolittle] had been advertised to speak himself. Gen'l S[herman] remained to the close of the meeting and I believe fully approved of nearly all the sentiments expressed by Judge D[oolittle]. I will show you a copy. — This afternoon Col. Giddings and myself were invited down to Gen'l Fairchilds to see, and take a glass of wine with, the old Gen. Col. G. and I were the only army officers there, although several celebrated citizens were present, amongst whom were Ex Gov. [Alexander W.] Randall, new 1st Asst. Post Master Genl. and others of less and equal note. — We passed an agreeable hour and half in the Genl's society and then went with him for a sail on the lakes. We sailed round about an hour in a little miniature steam boat, landing once on the opposite shore, and had a most delightful time. The Gen'l was charmed with the novelty of the conveyance and the beautiful scenery surrounding the lake. — He says

Madison is the most beautiful city he was ever in except Huntsville, Ala. — After the sail we walked back to the house with him when we bid him good life, as he is to leave this evening. He has won, during his stay here, the love of everybody by his sociability and the grace of his manners. — He talks fluently with anyone who addresses him and does not allow himself to be monopolized by any one person. — At Gen'l Fairchilds the politics of the country were discussed, and the Gen'l gave some of his views particularly on reconstruction he was quite enthusiastic. I have not time or space to relate them now, but they are substantially the same as those that President Johnson is now coming out [with]. He sustains the President's Mississippi policy, or rather his recent action in that state, of arming the militia and holding them responsible for the preservation of the peace and order of the state. Says he would select the best officers and soldiers of the late Confederate army, arming a few of them in their own communities, and hold them responsible for the preservation of the peace. He says that his experience shows that those who are now disposed to make the most trouble in the south are that class of person who have [sic] stayed at home and not smelt gun powder during the war etc., that this class of people are [sic] obnoxious to the late rebel soldiery and that he considers that civil affairs can be with more safety trusted to them, than to ¾ of those who stayed at home. Of course he accepts the loyal men of the south. I have already dwelt at considerable length on Gen'l Sherman, and will reserve some of his other views on the policy of reconstruction and other subjects, for another letter. —

One thing more and I must close. — Uncle Kendrick and Aunt N[ancy] have for the last two months been continually writing John to come home, that they want to see him very much and all that. — I have so far restrained him from going. — John is contented and happy here. His health never was so good any where else

*as it has been since he came out here. He has a fine
position, a good salary. If he goes home he loses his place
which he doesn't want to do. Still they importune him so
much to come that he feels he ought to go, he wants of
course to see them very much but still he feels he sacrifices
more than he can gain by going. . . . John wants to earn
his own living, to be independent of and not dependent
on his parents, who he knows are not in difficult
circumstances, but they won't let him be so. He would
have gone home two months ago if I hadn't kept him
back. I tell him he will never succeed in life if he has to
run home to see Pa and Ma every two or three months
and he agrees with me. — You know very well I would
like to see you very often and I know that you would like
to see me often, but it is impossible, and we don't make a
fuss over it, I come home whenever I can, and if it isn't
very often I can't help it. I can't sacrifice my position just
because I can't always be with you. — Please write to
Uncle K[endrick] or if he is in Belfast talk to him on this
subject that is if you agree with me and I am sure you
will. Tell him what you think about it. I presume that you
have as much love for me as they have for John, and I
know that I reciprocate in [sic] that love in as great if not
greater proportion than he does. — At any rate try and
convince them of their folly. John has determined to settle
in the west and if he goes home will only do so to come
right back again, and he knows he can't afford to be
running from New Hampshire to Wisconsin every three
months.*

Your son, Frank

In his letter of October 16, Frank discusses his future. He wants
to rejoin his regiment, and his reasons and logic for so doing
afford an interesting insight into the army way of doing things.

> Mustering and Disbursing Office
> Madison, Wis.
> October 16th 1865

Dear Father

Your several letters have been duly received, all of which relieved my apprehensions in regard to your health. I am rejoiced to hear that you are getting along so finely.

Col. Giddings received a telegram today from Ad'jt General of the army, enquiring "what objection, if any, is there to Lt. Dickerson's 5th Cav'l being relieved and ordered to his reg't where his services are urgently required." — Col. G. brought it to me, saying I was to dictate the answer, that is if I wanted to go. — It should be so, and if I didn't, he would answer that I couldn't be spared. This was very kind of him, indeed extraordinarily so for an officer of his rank; he appears to be quite attached to me, and I have a deep debt of gratitude for him, for this and many other kindnesses bestowed since I came here.

After thinking the matter over very carefully for some time, and taking a great many things into consideration which I cannot tell you of in this letter, I came to the conclusion that it was best, considering there was really no objection on account of official duties here, for me to go. — Knowing that no objection really existed on account of which I ought to be retained here, I couldn't conscientiously ask the Col. to say he couldn't spare me, when I knew he could. I told him I was ready to go the last of this month and he telegraphed back that my services could be spared here by the 1st of November. — So I shall probably receive an order in a few days ordering me to my reg't. —

Some of my reasons for desiring to go are these. —

1st It is a bad policy for an officer to kick against the requests of the Adjt. Genl's Dept. especially when he has been a long time away from his reg't and they relate to

170

his returning. — They know as well as we do here whether I can be spared or not.

2nd   An officer loses ground and reputation in his reg't by remaining a long time away from it. Officers get tired of doing the duties of absent officers, and some of them will grumble about it, and sometimes make a good deal of trouble to the absentee —

3rd   If I should succeed in staving off an order to my regt for the present, the probability is, the next order I should get, would not be to rejoin my reg't but would be an order to go before the Retiring Board, which I don't propose to do before I obtain my Captaincy, *if I can help it. — That is the way they serve officers who go on light duty on account of sickness and remain away a longer [time] than they think is necessary for them to get well. — Send them before the Retiring Board, who, if they are not perfect pictures of health, soon dispose of them. —*

4th   Last and not least I think it will be a better climate for me during the winter. I did not gain any here during Jan'y and Feb'y or March, in fact not until Spring was fairly open did I commence to improve. — The winters are severe here. I am afraid too much so for me. — It was through no effort of mine that this order came and, I think for the above, and many other reasons, it will be better to let things take their natural course. —

I will write again as soon as I receive my order. Continue to write me as usual at this place.

Love to all at home.

Aff'y Your Son
Frank

On October 12, 1865, a catastrophic fire swept Belfast. Originating in a boat-shop on the old common, it quickly spread to nearby storehouses filled with hay. Low tide, dry reservoirs, and only one of the two fire engines being fit for service enabled the fire to gobble up three houses before moving up Main Street.

Buildings on both sides soon blazed up, and sparks and flaming shingles ignited fires throughout southern Belfast. The flames engulfed street after street, as the Searsport fire engine and sailors from the U.S.S. *Tioga* helped Belfast's citizens battle the inferno. Having burned for 1½ hours, the fire climaxed at midnight, with Main Street devastated, and the northeast wind blowing off the water and fanning the flames. By 7 o'clock in the morning, the fire had died out, but 125 buildings over a 20-acre area lay in ashes. The fire caused $200,000 damage, only 40% insured. Some believed an arsonist set it, others that it was an accident. A public meeting called by the mayor provided relief for the homeless.[13]

Madison, Wis
Oct. 24th, '65

Dear Father

   I have received your letter giving an account of the great fire in "B"[elfast] which I read with greatest interest. I sympathize deeply with the good people of "B" in their hour of affliction, but I have no doubt that the generous citizens of "B" will see that they do not suffer long by reason of this great calamity. — I trust too that our "City Fathers" have at last realized the importance of an efficient fire department. The security of the past is no longer an argument in favor of indifferent fire engines and an unorganized Fire Dept., and that in the future they will have the city so prepared for conflagration that they will not be dependent upon the enterprise of the little village of Searsport for the safety of the city. Searsport may well be proud of her fire dept. — The importance of this subject cannot be overestimated.

   I received a telegram last night from the War Dept. saying that "orders have been received, relieving you from Mustering duty in the state of Wisconsin, and ordering you to join your 'Co.' when relieved at Nashville Tenn." This takes me completely by surprise as I expected to go to Washington or Cumberland Md. I do not know as

The Great Belfast Fire of October 12, 1865, as seen in an engraving by William M. Hall. The fire started at 10:30 p.m., reached its height by midnight, and finally died out at seven o'clock in the morning. The flames had covered 20 acres and destroyed 125 buildings. (Courtesy Belfast Museum)

*yet whether the whole reg't is to go there or whether it is
only a few companies. — My "Co" has heretofore been
with Gen'l Grant in Washington. I can't tell how I shall
like Nashville, but from all accounts the location will be
preferable to either of the other places. — I will write you
again as soon as I find out the nature of this change.
I shall probably receive my orders (officially) in a few
days. — Don't expect to leave here before the 4th of Nov.
Love to all. Direct to me at this place.*

Affe'y
Frank

Frank's next letter, four days later, discusses his new orders,
John's illness, and how "I long . . . to see you all again."

*Mustering and Disbursing Office
Madison, Wis.
Oct. 29th 1865*

Dear Father
    *Since last writing you I have received orders relieving
me from duty here on the 1st of Nov. — and ordering me
to rejoin my company at Nashville. — Four companies
"B" "D" "E" "M" are ordered to report for duty there to
Major Gen'l Mc[?]Thomas [*George M., Commanding
General, Department of Tennessee*]*, Gen'l Grant has
dispensed with all of his escort but our company (Capt.
Mason's) which he still retains. — Four companies under
command of Capt. Walker still remain on duty in
Cumberland M'd, and 3 companies with the Re'l
[Regimental] H'd Qurs are ordered to the Department of
Washington — This is the assignment of the reg't as made
by Gen'l Grant which will probably not be changed
during the coming winter, unless some unforseen
emergency arises to demand it.*
    I shall probably leave here on the 2d or 3d of Nov.

I shall send a box home by express, containing some articles of clothing which I shall not be likely to need this winter and which I haven't room to carry along with me. — John has been unwell for a few days (the first time since he has been here) but is out again today and is doing well. He had an attack of fever but has broken it up and appears to be coming out all right. It is quite unhealthy here this fall, the disease principally being Typhoid fever. —

It rained and stormed every day last week until Friday when it closed up with quite a little snowstorm, which lasted into Saturday. It is quite pleasant to witness the sun again. — Today (Sunday) being the first time we have seen it for a week. —

My accounts for the disbursement of public funds since my stay appear to have come out all right, leaving a balance of ten cents to my credit in the bank after final settlement. Some $80,000 have passed through my hands since I have been here, and it is quite gratifying to me to have it come out so straight I can assure you. —

Give my love to all at home.

I long for the time to come when I shall see you all again, but endeavor to wait patiently, believing it is for the best.

Direct your next letter to me "5th U.S. Cavalry Nashville Tenn" and please write soon, as I shall be anxious to get a letter from home soon after I get there.

> *Affectionately Your Son*
> *Frank*

As Frank prepares to leave for Nashville, his colleagues surprise him, and he is deeply moved, according to excerpts from his November 4 letter.

I have been relieved from duty here today and expect to leave here for Nashville tomorrow night (Sunday). I have this day sent home by express a box containing some articles of clothing etc. which I shall probably not want until next season. I don't know whether I shall be able to do duty with my company but shall try my best, — We have had about 3 weeks of as mean weather as I ever experienced. I trust it will be different in Nashville, for I must say it don't agree with me. . . .

. . . Sunday Morning

I commenced this letter last evening and while writing it I was interrupted by an invitation to call up to Col. Giddings' office in the story above mine, as some gentlemen there wished to see me. I laid this letter [to] one side and went, little dreaming at the time what I was wanted for. On arriving I met several gentlemen present, consisting of all the clerks in the office and the officers on duty here. — I was some what suspicious at seeing them altogether in the evening at the office (an unusual occurrence) but supposed they had met perhaps to say good bye etc. to me. Imagine my surprise when Mr. Blake who has been my chief clerk in the Mustering Dept. since I have been here came towards me with a box in his hand and addressing me by name in a neat and appropriate speech presenting me on behalf of the clerks of my office with a most elegant military sash, as a token of their love and esteem. — I was very much affected and surprised at this manifestation of their regard but managed to respond in a few brief and feeling words. I know of nothing in a long time that has affected me so much as this little scene did. — The sash was an elegant one, one of the finest I ever saw. It must have cost between 30 and 40 dollars and was just exactly what I wanted and needed. — It is a great gratification to me on leaving here to know that I carry with me the esteem of those with whom I have been officially associated and who have had opportunities to know me best. —

I leave here tonight. Col. Giddings goes with me to Chicago. [14]

Frank now speaks at length of his affection for his family, including the Judge, his "only parent," and of others for him, his journey to Nashville, and in conclusion, offers an excellent description of an army post of the time.

Head Qur's 5th Cav'y De't
Near - Nashville - Tenn.
Nov. 18th 1865

My dear Father
Your long letter of a recent date written at Rockland and filled with sentiments of endearments and affection was duly received soon after my arrival here and treasured, as only an affectionate and loving son can treasure such things from his dear parents, and brothers and sisters at home. — It is a great blessing for me to receive such kind words from an only parent and to know that a long absence from him does not estrange his love and concern or widen the kinds of affection which indissolubly link them together. May a kindly Providence extend his watchful care over us all, and may the coming of Spring see us all once more reassembled and reunited in that dear old place home. —
I left Madison on the night of the 5th inst., arriving in Chicago the following morning — Monday — at which place I remained during the day and night, leaving early Tuesday morning, traveling all day and arriving at Indianapolis, Ind. at 5 o'clock in the evening. Here I rested all night, and here I had the pleasure of meeting an officer formerly of my reg't but now on the retired list on account of losing one of his legs in one of Sheridan's great cavalry fights in the Valley of Virginia. Leaving I[ndianopoli]s the next morning — Wednesday — and traveling all day, I arrived in Louisville K'y at 5 in the evening without seeing any one I knew or meeting with an incident worthy of narration. Taking a good nights rest — which I relished after the fatigue of my journey —

I left Louisville early next morning and journeyed on towards Nashville, where I arrived at 6 o'clk in the morning, considerably tired and glad enough I had reached my journey's end. — I find that some of the officers had been at the hotel that day enquiring for me, and had left, and that they would come again. I did not however see any of them until the following day Friday at noon, when two of them came over for me in a carriage. — They were rejoiced to see me once more and not the less was I to see them. — I found out from them that our command was encamped about a mile from the city just across the Cumberland River in the little town of Edgefield. — I rode back with them and found both officers and men comfortably ensconced in comfortable modern quarters and barracks. — I can hardly describe to you my meeting with my old friend and companion in arms Capt. E. H. Leib now a Brevet Lieut. Colonel. — Wrapped in each others arms, we could not control our feelings and each gave way to a natural flow of tears, — fortunately for our dignity and for our sensibilities no one was near to witness the meeting or to mar the exhibition of our fraternal love. —

Col. Leib is in command of our detachment consisting of four companies of the Regt. —

I found the command right on the eve of moving — which we did a few days after — across the river into the Barracks which we now occupy on the Nashville side of the river and about the same distance from the city as we were before — one mile from the city. We now occupy the finest quarters and barracks in or about the city of Nashville formerly called the Heyde Femy (?) Pike Barracks, but changed by us to "Ash" Barracks in honor of the memory of the late Capt. Ash of the regiment who was killed in the great Wilderness campaign. The Officers' Quarters are in a large two story building with a veranda around it — the building containing eight rooms on each floor, all of the same size besides kitchen

MICHELE LEACH

The Dickerson home at the corner of Pearl and Cedar Streets in Belfast as it appears today, more than 140 years after Judge Dickerson purchased it from Thomas and Susan Marshall on October 18, 1850 for $1,600. The house was built in 1845.

sec[tion]. I have two rooms over a corner room and either of them as large as our sitting room — the rooms open into each other and each have an open fire place. The mens' quarters are also in large two story buildings, with porches around them, each company having a building by itself, the lower floors containing the company mess room, kitchen and washrooms — Water is connected into these building through pipes from the river. — These buildings are built so as to form a hollow square, forming our parade and drill ground. — In the center of the square is a tall flag staff from the top of which during the day floats "old glory" — The buildings are all whitewashed and present a very neat appearance, our whole camp is enclosed by a board fence whitewashed on both sides. — We also have besides what I have

179

*enumerated a Guard House, Adjutants Office, Officers
stables etc. Also all inside the enclosure, the stables for the
men's horses are outside distant several hundred yards.
There are only 6 officers present with the command,
making a very comfortable little family. We all mess
together in the same building our own quarters are in. —
Col Leib has appointed me Recruiting Officer for the
detachment, with an office in the city of N[ashville]. I
shall however continue to live out here for the present. Go
in the morning about 9 — and come out in the evening
at 4 — It's only a miles' ride any way, and I prefer living
out here with the officers to boarding in the city. — I
have been just as busy as a bee ever since I came here,
which accounts for my not writing home sooner. I am in
receipt of a long letter from Ellen which I shall endeavor
to answer very soon. The weather here has been rather
disagreeable ever since my arrival, our having had a
great deal of rain, it has been very mild and warm,
however I have not been here long enough yet to tell how
it will effect but am favorably inclined to think it will
prove beneficial.
Give my love to all, as soon as I get my quarters fixed
up and my Recruiting office fairly running I hope to have
more leisure and shall write oftener than I have so far.
Affy Your Son
Frank*

Frank soon becomes Quartermaster (the officer charged with
supplying clothing and subsistence for his troops) of his command as well as recruiting officer, "and the duties of both posi-
tions keep me busy all the time," he writes Judge Dickerson on
December 14. He has harsh words for Nashville in particular, and
Tennesseeans in general and finds Northern men superior to
Southern both physically and mentally.

*It is much more agreeable . . . than serving with a
company and being subject to all the details of a Company*

officer. I have been very successful in recruiting both as to members and quality of recruits. — We report directly to Gen'l Thomas (formerly our Colonel) now commanding the Military Division of Tenn. and are not subject to the orders of any intermediate commander. The General's Hd Qur's are in the city. He takes great pride in our little command and gives us all we ask for. —

We learn from Washington on the most reliable authority that our regiment is to be consolidated and sent to California in the spring —

I thought of you often on Thanksgiving Day and wished my self with you. We had a small party of ladies and gentlemen out from the city to dine with us, and had a very good dinner for a camp dinner. Some of the officers received boxes of nice things from their homes, but they all came too late for Thanksgiving day, although they [were] relished just as well afterwards.

The weather for the past week or 11 days has been wet and disagreeable until this morning, when it cleared off cold and clear. My impressions of Nashville were not favorably raised during the wet weather, the mud was dreadful. Nashville is the meanest and poorest city I have yet seen in the U.S. and the Tennessee people as a general thing are the most illiterate, and shiftless class of people I have yet fell [sic] in with in or out of my travels. Your exalted ideas of the character and people of this state would soon disappear, could you have an opportunity of studying and visiting them. — Its reputation consists in fictitious traditions and the fact that it was [Andrew] Jackson's home and final resting place.

Since I have been in recruiting service I have had a splendid opportunity of witnessing the difference in physique and intelligence between northern and southern men. When I have found one man from the north who couldn't write his name, I have found ten from the south. The difference in the physique of the two classes is much more marked and greater in favor of northern men. —

181

*Fortunately the most of the men I have enlisted are from the
north, soldiers discharged from the Volunteer Army etc.,
employees in the different dept's and men who have followed
the cause of the armies in some capacity or other since the
war began. The Tennessee recruits are the poorest of all. I
have enlisted a few good men from Northern Ala. and
Kentucky, the rest are all northern and western men. —
I have not time to write more now.*

Two weeks now pass and, sadly, Frank's time for writing letters is coming to an end. The faithful stream of letters to his father
abruptly ends with a last missive. Always a fighter, he clings to
the last to the hope of regaining his health.

December 31, 1865

Dear Father

*Christmas passed off very well with us here, although it
was by no means a home Christmas. Tomorrow, New
Year's day, I suppose will be the same. I am still busily
engaged nearly all the time with my various official duties.*

*I am sorry to say that my health does not improve in
this climate as rapidly as I expected. On the contrary
I do not think it agrees with me as well as that of
Wisconsin. The weather here varies a great deal, not
having three days of one kind of weather in succession —
Yet I struggle against all this with the energy of
desperation and am bound not to give up while it is
possible for me to keep about.*

*At the earliest opening of spring I shall certainly come
home and then we can consult about the future. It will
probably be impossible for me to remain in the army
after then on account solely of poor health, and I shall
seek, if my health will permit it, some less exposed
employment. I was in hopes that our regiment would go
to California in the spring in which event I should
probably have accompanied them, but the 1st Cavalry*

have been ordered there instead. —
I trust all are well at home, have been expecting a letter
for some time from Ellen —
My love to all

Frank

The young lieutenant stayed at his post until January, 1866, when he finally had to face the reality of impending death. He said goodbye to his officer friends at Nashville to return to Belfast to spend his final days with those he loved so dearly. One can imagine the despair of this gallant young officer, so full of courage, life, and deep and abiding love for his family, as he moved East in a race with death. He lost that race, but not by much.

After vainly consulting doctors in New York City and Boston, on February 17, 1866, at the age of 24, Frank Wilberforce Dickerson died in his father's arms on board a steamer in Boston Harbor, so close to, yet so far from, Belfast. The cause of death: apparently a combination of consumption (tuberculosis) and chronic diarrhea.[15]

Frank's pastor, Reverend Cazneau Palfrey of Belfast's Unitarian Church, paid moving tribute to the young soldier's courage:

> He faithfully and conscientiously devoted himself to the duties of the position he had assumed. Animated by a generous ambition to distinguish himself in his profession and to rise in it by his merits and services, he shirked from no efforts or perils in the way of duty. The natural ardor of his temperament prompted him to seek the most active and stirring scenes of military life, and he showed himself to be possessed of the soldierly qualities of courage, endurance and persistent will. He won the respect and confidence of his superiors, the esteem and love of his associates, and the attachment of all who were under his command. With characteristic energy and determination, he lingered until almost the last moment at the post of duty, less he might seem to leave the service for an insufficient reason, and finally retired almost by the command of his superior officers.[16]

The Unitarian Church (now known as The First Church) on Belfast's Church Street. It is reasonable to assume that Frank Dickerson's funeral was held here, although no records exist to substantiate that assumption. The minister at the time, Rev. Cazneau Palfrey, did pay tribute to Frank as noted in the accompanying text. (Collection of Doris Hall)

184

The Dickerson family plot in Belfast's Grove Cemetery. The headstones are: rear, from left — Maj. Frank W. Dickerson (Frank was brevetted as Captain, then Major, about a year after his death); Ellen L., the Judge's first wife and Frank's mother (she died when Frank was 2 years of age); Judge Dickerson; Jerrie, the 8-year-old son of the Judge and his second wife, Lydia Jane (known as Jane), whose stone is at far right; front, from left — Rev. L.M. Barrington, who married Judge Dickerson's third wife, Eliza, after the Judge's death in 1878; Eliza; Johnnie, the son of the Judge and Eliza, who died in his 12th year; and Ellen L. Leib (and her daughter, Laura), daughter of the Judge and Jane. Ellen's marriage to Col. Edward H. Leib ended in divorce.

EPILOGUE

More tangible tributes to Lieutenant Dickerson's military career came too late for him to enjoy them. Shortly before Frank's death, Lt. Col. Edward Leib, who had inadvertently omitted Frank's name from an earlier list, urged that the brevet rank of captain be conferred upon him, and General Thomas "approved and earnestly recommended" this action.[1] On July 4, 1866, Judge Dickerson wrote his old friend U.S. Senator Lot M. Morrill of Maine to the same effect, noting that Colonel Leib, who was to eventually fall in love with, and marry, Frank's half-sister, Ellen, was visiting the Dickersons from Nashville. Colonel W.H. Emory, commander of the 5th U.S. Cavalry, had also recommended a brevet captaincy, and General Grant endorsed his letter "Approved and recommended."[2] President Andrew Johnson not only signed the brevet captain's commission on April 2, 1867, but also brevetted Frank as a major![3]

On April 11, in a grim bureaucratic glitch, the War Department informed Brevet Captain Dickerson of this honor. Two days earlier, he had been sent his commission as brevet major. In both cases, he was asked to acknowledge receipt of the commission.[4]

Frank, of course, had been dead for over a year, his body at rest in Grove Cemetery in his beloved hometown of Belfast, the little city by the bay.

Williamsburg,
Han'r. C. House,
Antietam,
Sheppardstown,
Halltown,
Upperville,
Markham Station,
Amesville,
Fredericksburg,
Kelleys Ford,
Flemings Cross Roads,
Beverly Ford.

V.

1827.
1906.

Your most affectionate son "Frank"

Acknowledgments

My deep appreciation is due to my USM History Department colleague Diane Barnes, who alerted me to this project initially; to my research assistant and son-in-law Raymond M. Dunning, like Frank a Lieutenant in the U.S. Army, who prepared the military biographies for the "Who Was Who" directory; to Mary Anne Wallace of the Westbrook College Library, who unearthed a wealth of material on Frank's Westbrook Seminary student days; to Sue Wright of the Maine Law Library who researched the figures on Maine Supreme Judicial Court justices' salaries before and after the 1864 raise; to Linn and Bill Johnson of North Country Press, who have been supportive and helpful at every step of the process from idea to finished book; to my secretary Gloria Oliver, who typed the manuscript in the midst of many other Departmental duties and who proved nothing less than brilliant in her ability to translate my handwritten "chicken scratches" into flawless type; and last but not least, to Lucy Richardson to whom this book is dedicated, whose warm and helpful interest in the project begun by her of publishing her great-uncle Frank's letters has meant so much to me.

I must also acknowledge my debt to my USM history colleagues and the USM administration, for making possible the sabbatical leave that enabled me to complete a large part of "*Dearest Father*." Special thanks to my friend Professor Joel W. Eastman, USM historian, for a helpful and supportive reading of the finished manuscript.

—H.D.H.

NOTES ON SOURCES

While a citation in the Notes has been provided for every direct quotation, I have chosen not to furnish a citation for every factual or interpretive statement in the narrative connecting Frank Dickerson's letters.

Most descriptions of military campaigns and major battles such as Antietam and Chancellorsville, as well as such set-pieces as Lee's surrender at Appomattox, Lincoln's assassination and the Grand Review, are drawn from my earlier book *Brother Against Brother: Understanding the Civil War Era* (Portland: J. Weston Walch, 1977), now out of print.

Among a number of eminently useful sources of Civil War information, I'm particularly indebted to: E. B. Long (with Barbara Long), *The Civil War Day By Day: An Almanac, 1861-1865* (Garden City, N. Y.: Doubleday & Company, 1971), Mark M. Boatner III, *The Civil War Dictionary* (New York: David McKay Company, Inc., 1959), and Stephen Z. Starr, *The Union Cavalry in the Civil War* (Vol. I) *Fort Sumter to Gettysburg* (Baton Rouge: Louisiana State University Press, 1979).

And the historical narrative is informed from first to last by over thirty years of studying and teaching the Civil War.

On Civil War Belfast, the indispensable source is: Joseph Williamson, *History of the City of Belfast in the State of Maine* (Portland: Loring, Short and Harmon, 1877 [Vol. I]; Boston: Houghton, Mifflin, 1913 [Vol. II], (both volumes reprinted by New England History Press in collaboration with the Belfast Free Library, 1982).

ENDNOTES

INTRODUCTION

1.   This statement, written in Ruffin's last diary entry before he committed suicide on June 17, 1865, captures faithfully his long-standing attitude toward Yankees. (Quoted in Betty L. Mitchell, *Edmund Ruffin: A Biography* (Bloomington: Indiana University Press, 1981), p. 256.

2.   *Ibid.*, pp. 178-181.

3.   Roy P. Basler, Editor, *The Collected Works of Abraham Lincoln* (New Brunswick, N.J.: Rutgers University Press, 1953), VIII, p. 332.

4.   Robert Penn Warren, *The Legacy of the Civil War: Meditations on the Centennial* (New York: Vintage Books, 1964), p. 3.

5.   Quoted in Bruce Catton, *This Hallowed Ground* (Garden City): Doubleday & Company, Inc., 1956, p. 19; quoted in Carl Sandburg, *Abraham Lincoln: The War Years* (New York: Harcourt, Brace & Co., 1929), I, pp. 215, 221-22, 216.

6.   Quoted in H. Draper Hunt, *Brother Against Brother: Understanding the Civil War Era* (Portland: J. Weston Walch, 1977), p. 47.

7.   E.B. Long (with Barbara Long), *The Civil War Day by Day: An Almanac, 1861-1865* (Garden City, N.Y.: Doubleday & Company, 1971), p. 711, 718-19, 726.

CHAPTER I

1. Joseph Williamson, *History of the City of Belfast in the State of Maine* (Portland, Loring Short and Harmon, 1877. Reprinted by New England History Press, 1982), I, Chapter 1, p. 465. (This book is a treasure trove of information about every aspect of Belfast and its citizens' lives.)

2. R.H. Stanley and George O. Hall, *Eastern Maine and the Rebellion* (Bangor: R.H. Stanley & Company, 1887), p. 230.

3. Williamson, *Belfast*, I, p. 465.

4. Apropos of Dickerson's editorship, the *Belfast Republican Journal* reminisced on February 9, 1871:

> The old Belfast Journal bore a prominent part in the history of Waldo democracy. It was one of the first political newspapers that we read, and although not sympathizing even then with its politics, we always perused with pleasure the pungent and incisive leaders of [Benjamin] Griffin, and afterwards [George B.] Moore, and then of Dickerson, who has since donned the judicial garb. The Journal during all these years was the ablest democratic paper in the State— always sharp, pithy, witty and severe; and under the present able direction of W.H. Simpson, esq., it has lost none of its ability and pungency.

5. Williamson, *Belfast*, II (Boston: Houghton Mifflin, 1913), pp. 129-130.

6. William George Crosby, *Annals of Belfast for Half a Century: Early Histories of Belfast, Maine* (Camden: Picton Press, 1989), pp. 119, 141, 143.

7. *Ibid.*, p. 193.

8. Death notice, Colby University Commencement, 1879. Alfred Johnson (ed.), *Vital Records of Belfast, Maine to the Year 1892, Marriages and Deaths* (Portland: Maine Historical Society, 1919), I, p. 62; II, p. 528.

> The second Mrs. Dickerson's obituary appears in an unidentified clipping, almost certainly in the *Belfast Republican Journal*. Obituaries scrapbook, Penobscot Marine Museum, p. 41.

9. H. Hayford, *1860 Census, Belfast, Waldo County, Maine*.

> Eliza Berry Dickerson, whom the judge married on June 9, 1859, was a native of Bennington, Wyoming County, New York. Colby obituary *op. cit.*

10. Registrar's Records at Westbrook College reveal that Frank (with his surname consistently misspelled "Dickinson") studied at Westbrook Seminary for part of the Spring, 1858 term, then enrolled for all of the Fall term, 1858, Winter term, 1858-59, Spring term, 1859, Fall term, 1859 and Spring term, 1860. Subsequently a blank occurs in the record until 1862, by which time Frank had embarked on his Civil War career. *H.D.H.*

> His studies, which cost $7.00 per term (presumably he boarded in the community), included Algebra, Latin, Chemistry, Rhetoric, Arithmetic, Spanish, and French. He displayed rhetorical skills (could he have been a "chip off the old block?") at the June 15, 1859 Annual Exhibition, declaiming on the "Pleasures of Memory." Registrar's Records and Annual Exhibition program (Westbrook College Archives). *HDH.*

11. George F. Price, *Across the continent with the Fifth Cavalry* (New York: D. Von Nostrand Publisher, 1883), p. 496. (The tone of the biographical sketch

of Frank in this very useful regimental history suggests that the author knew Lieutenant Dickerson well. *HDH.*)

12. The Glazier quote appears in Stephen Z. Starr, *The Union Cavalry in the Civil War: Volume I: From Fort Sumter to Gettysburg* (Baton Rouge: Louisiana State University Press, 1979), p. 89. (This splendid opus is the definitive work on the subject. *HDH.*)

CHAPTER II

1. Quoted in Catton, *Hallowed Ground*, p. 26.

2. These observations about Civil War soldiers are based upon many years' Civil War reading and teaching. Classic works on the subject include, Bell I. Wiley, *Billy Yank and Johnny Reb* (Indianapolis: Bobbs, Merill Company, 1943, 1951, 1952); Catton, op. cit.; Catton, *Mr. Lincoln's Army* (Garden City, N.Y.: Doubleday & Company, 1951). *HDH.*

3. T. Harry Williams, *Lincoln and His Generals* (N.Y.: Alfred A. Knopf, 1952), p. 19. (This is an excellent source for sketches of Army of the Potomac commanding generals under whom Frank served. *HDH.*)

4. Quoted in Catton, *Mr. Lincoln's Army*, pp. 64-65.

5. *Ibid.*, p. 65.

6. Quoted in Stephen W. Sears, *George B. McClellan: The Young Napoleon* (N.Y.: Ticknor & Fields, 1988), p. 132. (This is the best biography of the controversial general. *HDH.*)

7. Starr, *Union Cavalry*, I, Chapter I; Douglas Southall Freeman, *R.E. Lee* (N.Y.: Charles Scribner's Sons, 1934), I, pp. 349, 360-61.

8. Slonaker to the author, October 25, 1991.

9. Starr, *Union Cavalry*, I, pp. 51-53, 59-60.

10. Quoted in *ibid.*, p. 60, fn. 34; quoted in Sears, *Young Napoleon*, p. 114.

11. Price, *Across the Continent*, p. 497.

12. *Ibid.*

13. Long, *Civil War Day by Day*, p. 235.

14. Probably Jonathan H. Fuller, deputy collector of Customs under Frank's father in 1858. *HDH.*

15. Possibly a medical leave authorization. *HDH.*

16. Quoted in Shelby Foote, *The Civil War: A Narrative: Sumter to Perryville* (New York: Simon & Schuster, 1958), I, p. 698.

17. McClellan quoted in Sears, *Young Napoleon*, p. 306. Alfred Pleasonton to Randolph B. Marcy, September 19, 1862, in *Official Records of the Union and Confederate Armies* (Washington: U.S. Government Printing Office, 1887), Series I, Vol. XIX, Part I, pp. 211-12.

18. Sears, *Young Napoleon*, p. 306; quoted in Stephen W. Sears, *Landscape Turned Red: The Battle of Antietam* (New Haven: Ticknor & Fields, 1983), p. 271. See *ibid* for preceding quote on Cavalry Division's role in the battle.

19. Sears, *Young Napoleon*, p. 306.

20. Quotations in Sears, *Landscape Turned Red*, pp. 314-15.

21. James M. McPherson, *Battle Cry of Freedom: The Civil War Era* (New York: Oxford University Press, 1988), p. 544.

22. Long, *Civil War Day by Day*, p. 269. The cautious McClellan admonished Pleasonton to eschew cavalry pursuit unless he recognized "a splendid opportunity to inflict great damage upon the enemy without loss to yourself" [!]. McClellan quoted in, Sears, *Young Napoleon*, pp. 321-22.

23. "List of battles in which Lieutenant Frank M. Dickerson late of 5th U.S. Cavalry participated" (Williams Barracks, Washington, D.C., March 8, 1866, attested to by James Hastings, Brevet Major and Adjutant, 5th U.S. Cavalry); Price, *Across the Continent*, p. 497.

24. Bruce Catton, *Glory Road* (Garden City, N.Y.: Doubleday & Company, 1952), p. 30.

25. Starr, *Union Cavalry*, I, p. 325.

26. Quoted in Shelby Foote, *The Civil War: A Narrative: Fredericksburg to Meridian*, Vol. II (New York: Random House, 1963), p. 38.

27. A large sheet-iron can filled with iron balls and fired from a cannon.

28. Quoted in *ibid.*, pp. 35-6.

29. Quoted in Hunt, *Brother Against Brother*, p. 79.

30. Willard Wallace, *Soul of the Lion: A Biography of General Joshua L. Chamberlain* (N.Y.: Thomas Nelson & Sons, 1960), p. 54.

31. Clifford Dowdey (Editor), *The Wartime Papers of Robert E. Lee* (Boston: Little, Brown, 1961), p. 380.

CHAPTER III

1. Benjamin Quarles, *Lincoln and the Negro* (New York: Oxford University Press, 1962), p. 140-41; apparently a Seward reminiscence quoted in F.B. Carpenter, *Six Months at the White House with Abraham Lincoln: The Story of a Picture* (New York: Harland Houghton, 1867), p. 269.

2. Quoted in, John L. Thomas, *The Liberator: William Lloyd Garrison: A Biography* (Boston: Little, Brown, 1963), p. 420.

3. *Belfast Republican Journal*, February 28, September 26, October 3, 1862. So strident did this Democratic newspaper become in its attacks on conscription that Editor William H. Simpson was indicted for giving aid and comfort to the Confederacy in an article on the draft (July 22, 1864) entitled "More Victims for the Slaughter Called For." Although acquitted, Simpson voluntarily suspended publication on December 2, 1864, promising to go back into print "as soon as a changed condition of the country and more encouraging business prospects should permit." The *Republican Journal* duly reappeared on July 20, 1866. Williamson, *History of Belfast*, I, pp. 355-56.

4. Quoted in Foote, *Civil War*, II, p. 129.

5. Quoted in *ibid.*, p. 146. See Catton, *Glory Road*, Chapter Two, for a vivid account of the "Mud March."

6. Quoted in Walter H. Hebert, *Fighting Joe Hooker* (Indianapolis: Bobbs-Merrill Company, Publishers, 1949), p. 180.

7. Quoted in Foote, *Civil War*, II, p. 232. See pp. 232-35 for an excellent character sketch of Hooker.

8. See Catton, *Glory Road*, pp. 156-172 for an excellent account of Hooker's army reforms.

9. *Ibid.*, p. 86.
10. Frank's half sister, attending Pemberton Square Young Ladies English and French School.
11. Starr, *Union Cavalry*, I, p. 339.
12. Price, *Across the Continent*, p. 497-98.
13. Starr, *Union Cavalry*, I, p. 343.
14. Quoted in Hebert, *Fighting Joe Hooker*, p. 186.
15. Starr, *Union Cavalry*, I, pp. 346-48.
16. Quoted in Foote, *Civil War*, II, p. 246. For an insightful assessment of the battle, see Starr, op. cit., pp. 347-50.
17. Price, *Across the Continent*, pp. 114-15.
18. Quoted in Hunt, *Brother Against Brother*, p. 80; McPherson, *Battle Cry of Freedom*, p. 639.
19. Starr, *Union Cavalry*, I, p. 352.
20. Quoted in *ibid.*, p. 353.
21. Quoted in *ibid.*, p. 355.
22. *Ibid.*, pp. 356-57.
23. Quoted in Hebert, *Hooker*, p. 196.
24. Quoted in Frank Vandiver, *Mighty Stonewall* (New York: McGraw-Hill Book Company, Inc., 1957), p. 494.
25. Quoted in Benjamin P. Thomas, *Abraham Lincoln: A Biography* (New York: Alfred A. Knopf, 1952), p. 370.
26. Emory M. Thomas, *Bold Dragoon: The Life of J.E.B. Stuart* (New York: Harper & Row, Publishers, 1986), pp. 217-20.
27. Freeman, *Lee's Lieutenant's* (New York: Charles Scribner's Sons, 1944), III, ch. 1.
28. Quoted in Starr, *Union Cavalry*, I, p. 379. An eyewitness to another cavalry charge might have been describing the 6th U.S. in action: "It is a thrilling sight to see these gallant men draw their sabres, and dash into those lines of steel. But it is like sending men to certain death. The officers are nearly all killed; the men are cut down by the score . . . and the shattered remnant that returns to us only tramples down our own men and increases the disorder already begun." *Ibid.*, f.n. 48, pp. 277-78.
29. Improperly called a ball, it was actually bullet (or cone)-shaped, with a hollow base, the invention of French Army Captain Minié. *HDH.*
30. Price, *Across the Continent*, p. 498.
31. Adelbert Ames (1835-1933), a Rockland, Maine, native and West Pointer, commanded the famous 20th Maine Regiment and had become a brigadier general of volunteers less than a month before Brandy Station. Division and corps command came to him later in the war, and he finished as a brevet major-general. During Reconstruction, he served successively as U.S. Senator from, and governor of, Mississippi. *HDH.*
32. Starr, *Union Cavalry*, I, p. 385.
33. Quoted in *ibid.*, p. 390. Starr's Union Cavalry contains a superb account of Brandy Station (see Ch. XIV). See also Samuel Carter III, *The Last Cavaliers* (New York: St. Martin's Press, 1979), Ch. 11 and Thomas, *Bold Dragoon*, Ch. XI.

CHAPTER IV

1. Quoted in Thomas, *Lincoln*, p. 383.
2. Lincoln quoted in Williams, *Lincoln and His Generals*, p. 260.
3. Quotations in Bruce Catton, *Gettysburg: The Final Fury* (Garden City, N.Y.: Doubleday & Company, Inc., 1974), pp. 88, 93.
4. Dr. Hunter's letter, National Archives.
5. Williamson, *History of Belfast*, pp. 465-75.
6. Long, *Civil War Day by Day*, p. 325.
7. Williamson, *History of Belfast*, pp. 475-92.
8. Probably William C. Emery of Belfast, age 32.
9. The United States Hotel.
10. The notorious New York Draft Riots (July 13-16, 1863) paralyzed the North's largest city. Governor Horatio Seymour, New York Peace Democrat, set the stage by challenging the federal government's right under the U.S. Constitution to enforce conscription. Mobs sprang up all over the city and coalesced into a horde of 50,000 largely Irish-Americans, anti-Negro as well as anti-draft. The mob overwhelmed the police, lit fires, torched a black church and orphan asylum (the war was being blamed on blacks), beat the police commissioner nearly to death, raided the office of the anti-slavery, pro-war N.Y. *Tribune*, sacked the home of the provost-marshal, chief draft enforcer, and caused $1,500,000 in property damage. Over a dozen people died in the riots. Eventually Union troops arrived fresh from Gettysburg and broke up the mob, with over 1,000 killed and wounded. Federal authorities postponed the draft until August 19; thus the rumor reported by Frank on the eighteenth. Mark M. Boatner III, *The Civil War Dictionary* (New York: David McKay Company, 1959), pp. 245-46.
11. Frank may well have had his photograph taken at Matthew Brady's celebrated Washington studio. *HDH.*
12. References to State elections.
13. Basler (ed.), *Collected Works of Lincoln*, VI, pp. 496, 497.
14. Once Frank captured two men with $12,000 on their persons on a mission to buy medicines for the Confederacy. They tried to bribe him with the full amount, but he sent them and their money to Fortress Monroe. Price, *Across the Continent*, p. 498.
15. General Butler had once served as military governor of New Orleans and caused a sensation by ordering that any woman of the city who insulted the flag or uniform of the U.S. would be treated as a common prostitute. The story goes that some Southern women reacted by pasting Butler's portrait on the bottom of their chamber pots. *HDH.*
16. The first "hero" of New Orleans was Flag-Officer (later Rear-Admiral) David Glasgow Farragut, whose ships captured the Crescent City in April, 1862. *HDH.*

CHAPTER V

1. Bruce Catton, *Grant Takes Command* (Boston: Little, Brown and Company, 1968), p. 124.

194

2.   Quoted in *ibid.*, p. 153.

3.   In 1836, the salary of an associate justice of the Maine Supreme Judicial Court was raised by $200 to $1,836. It took 28 years for the Legislature to raise the salary again, this time, on March 25, 1864, to $2,200. *HDH.*

4.   Long, *Civil War Day by Day*, p. 470, 471.

5.   Price, *Across the Continent*, p. 498.

6.   Quotations in Hunt, *Brother Against Brother*, p. 95.

7.   Boatner, *Civil War Dictionary*, p. 750.

8.   After the war, Holmes became successively chief justice of the Massachusetts Supreme Judicial Court and Associate Justice of the Supreme Court of the United States. *HDH.*

9.   Quoted in Thomas, *Lincoln*, p. 434.

10.   Quotation in James M. Merrill, *William Tecumseh Sherman* (Chicago: Rand McNally & Company, 1971), p. 266.

11.   On October 27, Union troops moved against the crucial South Side Railroad which angled west from Petersburg, only to be stopped by stiff Confederate opposition in the Battle of Hatcher's Run. Union losses numbered 1,758, with Rebel losses uncertain. *HDH.*

12.   Quotations in Long, *Civil War Day by Day*, pp. 563, 568.

13.   "Those Northern Democrats who opposed the Union's war policy and favored a negotiated peace." Boatner, *Civil War Dictionary*, p. 175.

14.   Stanley & Hall, *Eastern Maine and the Rebellion*, pp. 239-243; Williamson, *History of Belfast*, I, pp. 485-86.

15.   Probably a reference to William Pitt Fessenden, soon (January 1865) to return to the U.S. Senate from which he had resigned on July 1, 1864, to become Lincoln's Secretary of the Treasury. *HDH.*

CHAPTER VI

1.   In December, 1864, General Grant had placed General Benjamin F. Butler in command of a joint army-navy expedition to capture Fort Fisher. Troops landed to assault the Fort, the navy bombarded it, but Butler, fearing heavy casualties and an approaching Confederate force, withdrew his forces on the recommendation of his second-in-command, Maj. Gen. Godfrey Weitzel. *HDH.*

2.   Quoted in Long, *Civil War Day by Day*, p. 640.

3.   "For practical purposes brevet rank can be regarded as an honorary title, awarded for gallant or meritorious action in time of war, and having none of the authority, precedence, or pay of real or full rank." Boatner, *Civil War Dictionary*, p. 84.

4.   Quoted in Bruce Catton, *Grant Takes Command*, (Boston: Little, Brown, 1968, 1969), p. 464.

5.   Clara Harris, daughter of U.S. Senator Ira Harris of New York, was engaged to Major Rathbone. Rathbone received a deep arm wound from Booth's knife. The couple married and moved to Germany. Eventually Rathbone became insane, murdered his wife and ended his days in a mental institution.

6. Quoted in Ruth Painter Randall, *Mary Lincoln: Biography of a Marriage* (Boston: Little, Brown, 1953), p. 382.

7. Quoted in H. Draper Hunt, *Hannibal Hamlin of Maine: Lincoln's First Vice-President* (Syracuse: Syracuse University Press, 1969), p. 200.

8. For a description of this unfortunate episode, see ibid., pp. 195-98.

9. Booth began investing in Pennsylvania oil land in December, 1863 or January, 1864, and by September, 1864, had sunk $6,000 in such land. There is some evidence that despite his boasts to people like Frank, "His speculations . . . were a total loss." See George S. Bryan, *The Great American Myth: The True Story of Lincoln's Murder* (N.Y.: Carrick & Evans, 1940), p. 103.

CHAPTER VII

1. Quoted in Williamson, *History of Belfast*, I, p. 495.

2. *Ibid.*, footnote 1, p. 496.

3. For the older, pro-Johnson view, see William A. Dunning, *Reconstruction, Political and Economic* (1907), for more current historical thinking on Johnson and Reconstruction, see Eril L. McKitrick, *Andrew Johnson and Reconstruction* (1960), Kenneth M. Stampp, *The Era of Reconstruction, 1865-1877* (1965), and Eric Foner, *Reconstruction: America's Unfinished Revolution* (1988). *HDH.*

4. Quoted in Philip Van Doren Stern, *An End to Valor: The Last Days of the Civil War* (Boston: Houghton Mifflin Company, 1958), p. 343. Stern's book contains a splendid account of the Grand Review. See Chapter 23.

5. Horace Porter, *Campaigning with Grant* (N.Y.: The Century Co., 1897), p. 510. See pages 505-512 for another first-rate description of the Review.

6. Quoted in Stern, *An End to Valor*, p. 350.

7. Aabel Dickerson, the new baby, who apparently did not live to maturity.

8. Frank to "Dear Father," June 23, 1865.

9. Frank to "Dear Father," July 17, 1865.

10. Frank to "Dear Father," July 29, 1865.

11. Frank to "Dear Father," August 14, 1865.

12. Frank to "Dear Father," September 11, 1865.

13. Williamson, *History of Belfast*, I, pp. 726-27.

14. Frank to "Dear Father," November 4, 1865.

15. The historian of the 5th U.S. Cavalry speaks of Frank developing at Leonardtown, Maryland, a "stubborn cough which, in conjunction with the disease contracted in the Peninsular campaign of 1862 [presumably dysentery], finally ended his brief but eventful and brilliant career." Price, *Across the Continent*, p. 498; The *Vital Records of Belfast, Maine to the Year 1892*, attributes his death to "chronic diarrhea." Alfred Johnson (Editor), *Vital Records of Belfast, Maine to the Year 1892, Volume II; Marriages and Deaths* (Portland: Maine Historical Society, 1919), p. 528. But Colonel W.H. Emory, commanding 5th U.S. Cavalry, also attributed Frank's death to the consumption. *Emory to John A. Rawlins*, June 24, 1866, National Archives.

16. Quoted in Price, *Across the Continent*, p. 499.

EPILOGUE

1. Leib to Secretary of War Edwin M. Stanton, January 15, 1866, National Archives.
2. Dickerson to Morrill, July 4, 1866; Emory to General John A. Rawkins, June 24, 1866, *ibid.*
3. Presidential Commission, April 2, 1867, *ibid.*
4. J.C. Kelton, Assistant Adjutant General to Brevet Major Frank W. Dickerson and Brevet Captain Frank W. Dickerson, April 9, 11, 1867. National Archives.

WHO WAS WHO IN FRANK DICKERSON'S LETTERS

Abbreviations

AAG   Asst. Adjutant General
AG   Adjutant General
AIG   Assistant Inspector General
IG   Inspector General
RA   Regular Army
USMA   United States Military Academy
VOLS   Volunteers

The following capsule biographies identify those individuals mentioned in Frank's letters who could be readily identified. In several cases, birth and/or death dates were not available in the sources utilized.

ANDERSON, HUGH J. (1801 - 1881)
Hugh J. Anderson, a self-made grocer from Belfast, who served a term in Congress and was Democratic governor of Maine from 1844- 1847. Governor Anderson had the reputation of a shrewd political manager in the mould of his friend Martin Van Buren.

ASH, JOSEPH P. (18? - 1864)
Captain Joseph P. Ash, of Pennsylvania, appointed 2nd Lt, 5th Cav. in April 1861. Promoted 1st Lt, 1862, then Captain in Sept. 1863. Participated in Virginia Peninsula and Maryland campaigns. Wounded at Little Washington; killed at Battle of Todd's Station on 8 May 1864.

AVERELL, WILLIAM WOODS (1832 - 1900)
General William Woods Averell, of New York, USMA 1855. Served at the Cavalry School at Carlisle Barracks. Was acting AG under General Porter at First Manassas. Appointed Colonel of the 3rd Pennsylvania Cav., commanding at Sharpsburg and Fredericksburg. Appointed Brigadier General (Vols.) 26 Sept 1862, and then commander of the 2nd Cavalry Division, winning at Kelly's Ford. Brevetted Major General, he resigned 18 May 1865.

BADEN, JAMES T.
1Lt. James T. Baden, of Maryland, was appointed 2nd Lt., 5th Cav., 17 July 1862. Promoted 1Lt. 2 Nov 1863; resigned 12 September 1864.

BRECKINRIDGE, JOHN CABELL (1821 - 1875)
Kentuckian Breckinridge served in Congress, as Vice-President of the United States (1857-61) and Southern Democratic Presidential nominee in 1860. Confederate general from 1861-65, he served briefly at the end of the war as Confederate Secretary of War.

BUFORD, JOHN (1826 - 1863)
General John Buford, of Kentucky, USMA 1848. Original Captain of 2nd Cav. Promoted Brigadier General 27 July 1862. Wounded at Second Manassas. Chief of Cavalry in Maryland Campaign. At Gettysburg, ordered his Brigades in opposition to A. P. Hill's Corps and established the Union line, stemming certain defeat. Died of typhoid.

BUTLER, BENJAMIN FRANKLIN (1818 - 1893)
General Benjamin Butler, of N.H., was Brigadier General of Massachusetts Militia, lifted blockade of Washington with the 8th Mass. First Vol. Major General appointed by Lincoln. Defeated at Big Bethel, later successful on Hatteras Inlet, and entering New Orleans. Was vilified as the military governor, and removed in 1862. He commanded the Army of the James and was ineffective at Bermuda Hundred. Butler was removed from command of the Army of the James as a result of his failure to capture Fort Fisher in December 1864. He resigned his commission on 30 November 1865. Butler served as Congressman from, and Governor of, Massachusetts after the war.

CHURCHILL, WILLIAM HARVEY (18? - 1866)
1Lt. William Churchill, of Indiana, served from 1855 to 1864 as an enlisted man. He was appointed 2nd Lt., 5th Cav. on 7 June 1864; and 1Lt. on 3 August 1865. Brevetted Captain for gallantry during Appomattox campaign. Died on 20 August 1866.

CUNNINGHAM, GEORGE A.
Major George A. Cunningham, of Georgia, USMA class of 1857, was brevetted 2nd Lt. of 2nd Cav., then 5th Cav. Oct. 1858. Resigned 27 Feb. 1861, and joined the Confederacy, serving as an officer of artillery and infantry.

CUSTER, GEORGE ARMSTRONG (1839 - 1876)
General George Custer, of Ohio, USMA 1861. Carried dispatches for General Winfield Scott; then a staff officer to McClellan and Pleasanton until 1863. Assigned a Brigade command 29 June 1863 in Kilpatrick's Division, with the rank of Brigadier (Vols). Fought in all cavalry battles with distinction, cutting off Lee's last escape at Appomattox. Promoted to full Major General of Volunteers in 1865, then in 1866 appointed Lt. Col. of the 7th Cav., commanding until his death at Little Big Horn, 25 June 1876.

DAVIS, HENRY WINTER (1817 - 1865) A lawyer from Maryland, former Whig and Know Nothing, he served in Congress from 1855-1861, and from 1863 until his death. Davis was a leader of the Radical Republicans in Congress and a harsh critic of what he deemed the soft Reconstruction policy of Presidents Lincoln and Johnson.

DENNEY, JEREMIAH (18? - 1869)
1Lt. Jeremiah C. Denney, of Ireland, was appointed 2nd and 1Lt., 5th Cav. on 17 July 1862. Brevetted Captain on 19 Oct. 1864 for gallantry at Cedar Creek. Died 12 June 1869.

DOOLITTLE, JAMES ROOD (1815-1897)
A native New Yorker and a Democrat until he converted to the new Republican Party over the slavery in the territories issue, Doolittle moved to Wisconsin in 1851, served three years as a judge until becoming a U.S. Senator in 1857. He served in the Senate until 1869. Doolittle returned to the Democratic Party but lost the 1871 race for governor of Wisconsin.

DRUMMOND, THOMAS (18? - 1865)
Capt. Thomas Drummond, of Iowa, appointed 2nd Lt. 2nd Cav. on 26 April 1861, than 1Lt. on 30 May that year. Became Captain in the 5th Cav. 17 July 1862, and was killed in action at Five Forks, Va., 1 April 1865.

ELLSWORTH, EDWARD AUGUSTUS (18? - 1881)
1Lt. Edward Ellsworth, of Maine, was appointed 2nd Lt. then 1Lt. of the 11th Infantry on 24 Oct. 1861. He was brevetted Captain 1 Aug. 1864 for gallantry at the Battle of the Wilderness. He died 20 Feb. 1881.

FAIRCHILD, LUCIUS (1831 - 1896)
General Lucius Fairchild, born in Ohio but raised in Wisconsin, first enlisted, then elected Captain of 1st Wisconsin. Became Lt. Col. of 2nd Wisconsin, the "Iron Brigade". Distinguished himself at Second Manassas and Sharpsburg. Promoted to Colonel 1 Sept. 1862. Was wounded on the first day of Gettysburg, promoted then to Brigadier General, and saw no more service. Resigned in November 1863. Served as Governor of Wisconsin and Minister to Spain in post-war years.

FLANDERS, DAVID P.
Dr. David P. Flanders, a homeopathic physician, graduated from Harvard Medical School in 1857 and set up his practice in Belfast in 1858.

GIDDINGS, GROTIUS REED (18? - 1867)
Lt. Col. Grotius Giddings, of Ohio, was Captain in 23 Ohio Infantry, then Major 14th Infantry 14 May 1861. Promoted Lt. Col. 18 May 1864, in command of the 16th Infantry. Brevetted Col. for gallantry at Gettysburg 13 March 1865. Died June 21, 1867.

GIDDINGS, JOSHUA REED (1795 - 1864)
Born in Pennsylvania but raised in New York and Ohio, "Josh" Giddings gained fame as a longtime (1838-59) abolitionist Congressman from the Western Reserve District of Ohio. First a Whig, then a Free-Soiler, then a Republican, Giddings died as U.S. Commissioner to Canada in 1864.

GRAHAM, LAWRENCE PIKE (1815 - 1905)
General Lawrence Graham, of Virginia, appointed directly into the Army in 1837. Promoted August 1861 to Brigadier General (Vols.). Assigned June 1862 as Chief of Cav. Annapolis. Became Colonel of 4th U.S. Cav. in 1864, retiring in December of 1870.

GREGG, DAVID McMURTIE (1833 - 1916)
General David Gregg, born Huntington Pa., USMA 1855. January 1862 appointed Colonel of 8th PA. Cav., serving in the Peninsular and Antietam campaigns. Commanded a division at Chancellorsville and at Gettysburg. Resigned on 3 Feb. 1865; died 7 Aug. 1916.

HALLECK, HENRY WAGER (1815 - 1872)
General Henry Wager Halleck, of New York, USMA 1839. At the outset of war in 1861, he was recommended for appointment as Major General, which he received Aug. 19, 1861. Relieved Frémont at St. Louis and reorganized the Dept. of the Missouri. His slow reaction in moving to Corinth after Shiloh allowed the Confederate withdrawal. Moved to Washington to command all the armies (General-in-Chief). Was an incapable leader, shifting responsibility and blame to others. Demoted March 1864 to chief of staff.

HAMLIN, HANNIBAL (1809 - 1891)
Born in Paris Hill, Maine, he studied law, served as speaker of the Maine House, Congressman (1843-47), Governor of Maine (January, 1857), U.S. Senator (1848-61, 1869-81) and Vice President of the United States (1861-65). Hamlin was a Democrat until 1856 when he converted to Republicanism. He strongly opposed slavery expansion. After he left the Senate in 1881, he served briefly as U.S. Minister to Spain. President Lincoln's role in Hamlin's replacement as Vice President by Andrew Johnson long remained controversial and conjectural, but historians today believe Lincoln engineered the change.

HANCOCK, WINFIELD SCOTT (1824 - 1886)
General Winfield Scott Hancock, of Pennsylvania, USMA 1844. Appointed Brigadier General (Vols.) in September 1861, and took part in Peninsular and Maryland campaigns. Promoted Major General 29 Nov. 1862, distinguishing himself at Fredericksburg. Ordered the line at Cemetery Ridge secured at Gettysburg, costing Lee the campaign. Fought at Petersburg, Wilderness, Spotsylvania, Cold Harbor, Reams Station and Boydton Plank Road. Promoted Brigadier General (U.S.) 1864. Hancock was Democratic Presidential nominee in 1880.

HARRIS, EDWARD
1Lt. Edward Harris, of Virginia, was appointed 2nd Lt., 5th Cav. on 7 June 1864, after serving as an enlisted man. Promoted to 1Lt. 29 Sept. 1864; brevetted Captain in 1864 for gallantry at Winchester. Resigned 31 Oct. 1866.

HASTINGS, JAMES
1Lt. James Hastings, of England, was appointed 2nd Lt., 5th Cav. on 17 July 1862. Promoted 1Lt. 25 Sept. 1863. Was brevetted Captain in 1864 for gallantry at Winchester, Va., then to Major for gallantry at Dinwiddie Court House, Va. Retired 22 Dec. 1868.

HINKS, EDWARD WINSLOW (1830 - 1894)
General Edward Hinks, of Maine, became Colonel of 19th Mass Infantry. Wounded at Glendale, and twice at Sharpsburg. Promoted 29 Nov. 1862 to Brigadier General, serving on Courts Martial until 1864. Commanded Negro Division of the XVIII Corps in Petersburg offensive. Resigned in 1865, but reappointed in the Regular Army as Lt. Col. of the 40th Inf. Brevetted Major General (Vols.) and Brigadier (Regular) he retired in 1870.

KEYES, ERASMUS D. (1810 - 1895)
Erasmus D. Keyes was a Maine West Pointer (1832), where he taught after graduation. Keyes served as aide and military secretary to U.S. Army General-in-Chief Winfield Scott and commanded a brigade in the first Battle of Manassas (Bull Run), July, 1861. That August he became a Brigadier General of volunteers. He was Commander of the IV Corps of the Army of the Potomac, and Major General (Vols.), when Frank met one of his staff officers. General Keyes later saw fighting in the Peninsula campaign, winning a Regular Army brevet as Brigadier General after the Battle of Seven Pines (May, 1862). He resigned his commissions on May 6, 1864.

KILPATRICK, HUGH JUDSON (1836 - 1881)
General Hugh Judson Kilpatrick, of New Jersey, USMA 1861. First Regular officer to be wounded in action, at Big Bethel. Became Colonel of 2nd N.Y. Cav, then Brigadier General (Vols.). He took part in every important Cavalry action in the Eastern theater, including Beverly Ford, Stoneman's Raid, and Gettysburg. Led Richmond Raid, wounded in Atlanta campaign. Promoted to Major General (Vols.) 19 June 1865, resigning soon thereafter.

LEE, FITZHUGH (1835 - 1905)
Nephew of Confederate Generals Robert E. Lee and Samuel Cooper, Fitz Lee became an outstanding cavalry commander, serving under Jeb Stuart, commanding the Army of Northern Virginia's cavalry division at the very end of the war and attaining the rank of Major General. After the war, Lee served as governor of Virginia, as a diplomat to Cuba and a blue-coated Major General of volunteers in the Spanish-American war. He died with his name on the U.S. Army list of retired regular army Major Generals.

LEIB, EDWARD HENRY (18? - 1892)
1Lt. Edward Leib, of Pennsylvania, was appointed 2nd Lt., 2nd Cav., 26 April, 1861, then 1st Lt. that June. Was brevetted Captain 5th Cav. 13 June 1862 for gallantry at Old Church, Va. Brevetted Major 1 April 1865 for gallantry at Five Forks; Lt. Col. for gallantry and Service during the war that same day. During the war, he participated in action at Gaines Mill, Peninsula evacuation, South Mountain and Antietam, and a skirmish near Shepherdstown. He participated in Kelly's Ford, Fredericksburg, Brandy Station, and Fleming's Cross Roads. Colonel Leib eventually married Frank's half-sister, Ellen.

MARSTON, GILMAN (1811 - 1890)
General Gilman Marston, of New Hampshire, three-time congressman, recruited and led 2nd N.H. at First Bull Run. Promoted Brigadier General before Fredericksburg. Established Point Lookout pen prison camp after Gettysburg. Involved in Union disaster at Cold Harbor, commanding a Brigade in "Baldy" Smith's XVIII Corps. Resigned 20 April 1865.

MASON, JULIUS WILMOT (18? - 1882)
1Lt. Julius Mason, of Pennsylvania became a 2nd Lt., 2nd Cav. on 26 April 1861, then 1st Lt. that June. Promoted Captain December 1862. Brevetted Major 9 June 1863 for gallantry at Beverly Ford. Brevetted Lt.Col. that August for gallantry at Brandy Station.

McDOWELL, IRVIN (1818 - 1885)
Irvin McDowell, West Pointer, 1838, Mexican War veteran. Catapulted from Major to Brigadier General, U.S.A. McDowell commanded the Union Army whipped at Bull Run in July, 1861, the Civil War's first major battle. When Frank mentions him, he had just turned in a lack-luster performance at III Corps, Army of Virginia, commander at Cedar Mountain and 2nd Bull Run (Aug. 1862). McDowell was one of the war's hard-luck generals. He never commanded troops in the field after 2nd Bull Run.

MEADE, GEORGE GORDON (1815 - 1872)
General George Meade, born Cadiz, Spain, USMA 1835. Made Brigadier General of Vols., and commanded a Pennsylvania Brigade. Fought in Seven Days Battle, 2nd Manassas, South Mountain and Sharpsburg. Commander, Third Div., I Corps, Left Grand Division, at Fredericksburg. Led V Corps at Chancellorsville. Commanded Army of the Potomac 28 June 1863. Prevailed at Gettysburg. Appointed Regular Army Major General 7 July 1863 and commanded Army of the Potomac for the rest of the war.

MERRITT, WESLEY (1834 - 1910)
General Wesley Merritt, of New York, USMA 1861. Became Aide de Camp to General Cooke, and then General Stoneman in 1862. Commanded reserve Cav. brigade in Chancellorsville raid. Promoted 29 June 1863 to Brigadier General, leading his brigade in Buford's division during Gettysburg. Brevetted Major General 1 April 1865. Was second in command under Phil Sheridan at Appomattox. After the war he commanded the 5th Cavalry and various military departments. He attained Major General (U.S.) in 1895, later serving in the Philippines during the Spanish-American War.

MIX, JOHN (18? - 1881)
Lt. John Mix joined the N.Y. volunteers as a private, was appointed 2nd Lt., 2nd Cav. 14 Aug. 1862, then later a Major of the 3rd N.Y. Cav. in September of that year. Became Lt. Col. of Vols. in April 1862, then resigned to become a 1st Lt. of 2nd Cav. He was promoted Captain 19 Oct. 1865, and Major in 1881, serving almost until his death in October of that year.

MORRILL, LOT MYRICK (1813 - 1883)
Born in Maine, Morrill, a lawyer, served in the Maine Legislature before being elected governor of Maine in 1857. He took Vice President-elect Hamlin's U.S. Senate seat in 1861, serving until he lost the seat to Hamlin in 1869. But he filled the late William Pitt Fessenden's Senate seat that same year and served until 1876, when he became President Grant's Secretary of the Treasury.

MOYLAN, MILES
2nd Lt. Myles Moylan, of Massachusetts, appointed 2nd Lt. 5th Cav. on 19 Feb. 1863. Dismissed 20 Oct. 1863. Reappointed 1st Lt. 4th Mass. Cav. 25 Jan. 1864, then Captain in December. He was brevetted Major (Vols.) for gallantry during Virginia Campaign. Won the Medal of Honor at Bear Paw Mountain, Mont., in 1877.

NICKELS, LUCY A.
Mrs. Lucy A. Nickels, Frank's "Aunt Lucy," was wife to sea captain David A. Nickels.

OWENS, WESLEY (18? - 1867)
Capt. Wesley Owens, of Ohio, USMA class of 1856, was 2nd Lt. of 2nd Cav., promoted to 1st Lt. on the eve of the Civil War. Promoted Captain 15 Jan. 1862. Served as Lt. Col., AIG until 1863, then Col. (for gallantry) of the 8th Ohio Cav. until June, 1865.

PENDLETON, GEORGE HUNT (1825 - 1889)
Ohio-born, lawyer Pendleton was a congressman when he ran for Vice President on the 1864 Democratic ticket with General McClellan. Unlike his running mate, he vociferously opposed the war. After the war he served a term in the U.S. Senate and died as Minister to Germany.

PLEASANTON, ALFRED (1824 - 1897)
General Alfred Pleasanton, of Washington, D.C., USMA 1844. Served in 2nd Cav. in defense of the Capital 1862. Promoted to Brigadier General after Peninsula campaign. Directed the Union Cav. at Brandy Station, thus "making the Union Cavalry". Promoted to Major General (Vols.) 22 June 1863. Relieved of command 25 March 1864.

RANDALL, ALEXANDER WILLIAMS (1819 - 1872)
Abolitionist Alexander Randall served as Wisconsin's Republican governor in the early war years. A native New Yorker, he moved to Wisconsin in 1840. He changed parties frequently, beginning as a Whig, becoming a Wisconsin Democrat, then a Free-Soiler, then a Democrat again, finally a Republican. After his governorship (1858-1862), he served as U.S. Minister to the Vatican, and Andrew Johnson's Postmaster General.

REYNOLDS, JOHN FULTON (1820 - 1863)
General John Reynolds, born Lancaster Pa., USMA 1841. Served as Commandant of Cadets USMA. 29 Nov. 1862 promoted Major General, offered Command of Army of Potomac after Chancellorsville, but declined. Commanded I Corps at Fredericksburg. Occupied Gettysburg, putting his Corps on Road northwest of town. Killed by a sniper.

ROSECRANS, WILLIAM STARKE (1819 - 1898)
General William Rosecrans, of Ohio, USMA 1842. Resigned 1854, reappointed 1861 as Colonel of Engineers under McClellan. Commanded a Brigade at Rich Mountain; his success against Robert E. Lee led to the birth of West Virginia. Captured Chattanooga, Tenn. as commander of the Army of the Cumberland, but his defeat at Chickamauga in Sept. 1863 finished his career. Was later appointed Commander, Dept. of Missouri, resigning in 1867.

SICKLES, DANIEL EDGAR (1819 - 1914)
General Daniel Sickles, of New York, was appointed Brigadier General (Vols.), 3 Sept. 1861. Promoted Major General 29 Nov. 1862. Fought on the Peninsula and at Sharpsburg. Commanded Division at Fredericksburg. Deployed his units in the Peach Orchard at Gettysburg, resulting in the destruction of the III Corps, and the loss of his leg. He was relieved of his command.

STONEMAN, GEORGE (1822 - 1894)
General George Stoneman, of New York, USMA 1846. Was third ranking Captain of 5th Cav., later promoted to Major. Was made Chief of Cavalry of the Army of the Potomac, and promoted to Brigadier, then Major, General on 16 March 1863. Commanded 3rd Corps at Fredericksburg, and was captured in the raid on Andersonville, 31 July 1864. Retired 1871.

SWEATMAN, ROBERT
1Lt. Robert Sweatman, of England, was appointed 2nd Lt. 5th Cav. on 17 July 1862, and 1st Lt. on 3 July 1863 for gallantry at Gettysburg. He was brevetted Captain on 10 May 1864 for gallantry and meritorious service at Beaver Dam Va.

TAYLOR, ALFRED B.
1Lt. Alfred B. Taylor, appointed 2nd Lt., 5th Cav. on 31 October 1863. Promoted to 1st Lt. 12 Sept. 1864. Brevetted Captain for gallantry through campaign ending with Lee's surrender.

THOMAS, GEORGE HENRY (1816 - 1870)
General George Thomas, of Virginia, USMA 1840. One of the first Majors of the 2nd Cav. in 1855. Commanded brigade under Patterson, made Brigadier General (Vols.) on 17 August 1861, then Major General (Vols.) on 25 April 1862. At Chickamauga he earned the sobriquet "Rock of Chickamauga". After his great victory at Nashville, he was appointed Major General (Regular), 16 Jan. 1865. He died in command of the Division of the Pacific on 28 March 1870.

205

URBAN, GUSTAVUS (18? - 1871)
1Lt. Gustavus Urban, of Prussia, was appointed Captain assistant AG (Vols.) in September 1861, after serving as an enlisted man in 2nd Cav. Appointed 2nd Lt., 5th Cav., 17 July 1862. Commanded Regiment from 4 Sept. to 3 Dec. 1864. Brevetted Captain 9 June 1863 for gallantry at Beverly Ford, then Major, 28 July 1864 for gallantry at Deep Bottom.

VALLANDIGHAM, CLEMENT LAIRD (1820 - 1871)
A noted Ohio Democrat, Vallandigham's name became synonymous with "Copperheadism", the Northern peace movement. A congressman at the outset of the war, Vallandigham opposed the war and all its measures. Arbitrarily arrested and convicted by a military court lacking jurisdiction, he was exiled to the Confederacy, but receiving a cool reception there, he went to Canada. He was whipped in the 1864 Ohio gubernatorial election. Practicing law after the war, he mortally wounded himself with a pistol in a freak courtroom accident.

WALKER, LEICESTER
Captain Leicester Walker, of Ohio, was appointed 2nd Lt., 2nd Cav. on 8 May 1861; became 1st Lt. 15 Jan. 1862. Brevetted Captain 9 June 1863 for gallantry at Beverly Ford. Brevetted Major for gallantry at Yellow Tavern. Discharged 30 December 1871.

WEITZEL, GODFREY (1835 - 1884)
General Godfrey Weitzel, of Ohio, USMA 1855. Was appointed in 1862 as chief of engineers under Butler's expedition against New Orleans. Promoted 29 August 1862 to Brigadier General (Vols.), commanding the XVIII Corps and the XXV Corps, Army of the James, making Major General (Vols.) on 17 November 1864.

WHITE, ANSEL LOTHROP (1835-1910)
A Belfast native, White enlisted in the 19th Maine Regiment in 1862, turned in an excellent war record and mustered out in 1865 as a Brevet Major. He pursued a business career after the war in Belfast, Boston and, for 35 years, in New York City, retiring to Belfast four years before his death.

WHITE, RUSSELL (1844 - 18?)
Russell White, a Belfast M.D., born 1844, was hospital steward of the 20th Maine Regiment in 1862 and 1863 before qualifying as a physician.

WILLIAMS, SETH (1822 - 1866)
General Seth Williams, of Maine, USMA 1842. Brevetted Captain at Cerro Gordo, served as adjutant at USMA from 1850 - 1853. Promoted to Major August 1861, Brigadier General (Vols.) the next month. He served as AG of the Army of the Potomac until March 1864, and was IG under Grant, serving until 1866.

WILSON, JAMES HARRISON (1837 - 1925)
General James Wilson, of Illinois, USMA 1860. Distinguished "Boy General". Topographical engineer in winter 1861-1862, became Aide de Camp to McClellan during Maryland campaign. In Vicksburg campaign was IG of Army of Tennessee. On Oct. 30, 1863 promoted to Brigadier General (Vols.) only officer of Grant's staff ever promoted to troop command. Assigned as Chief of Cavalry Bureau in Washington. Commanded division in Sheridan's cavalry through Richmond campaign into the Shenandoah Valley. Organized a corps in Western theater which he commanded during destruction of John B. Hood's Army of Tennessee at Franklin and Nashville. In a spectacular cavalry raid, he captured Selma, Alabama, April 2, 1865. Was made Major General (Vols.) ranking from 6 May 1865. Discharged 1870.

WILSON, ROBERT P.
1Lt. Robert P. Wilson, of Pennsylvania, was appointed 2nd Lt., 5th Cav. 1 June 1863. Served as Aide de Camp to Brigadier General Merritt. Promoted 1st Lt., May 1864; then Captain for gallantry at Beaver Dam Station on 10 May 1864. Resigned 29 July 1876, later serving as U.S. Consul, Moscow.

SOURCES

Heitman, Francis B., *Historical Register and Dictionary of the United States Army From Its Organization, September 29, 1789 to March 3, 1903* (Washington: U.S. Government Printing Office, 1903) 2 vols.

Sifakis, Stewart, *Who Was Who in the Civil War* (New York: Facts on File Publications, 1988).

Warner, Ezra J., *Generals in Blue: Lives of the Union Commanders* (Baton Rouge: Louisana State University Press, 1964).

Warner, Ezra J., *Generals in Gray: Lives of the Confederate Commanders* (Baton Rouge: Louisiana State University Press, 1959).

INDEX

Abbott, Nehemiah, 152
Abolitionists, 37, 39
Adams, Charles Francis, Jr., 26, 47
Alabama, C.S.S., 110
Allen, Miss, 74–76
Alexandria, 19–21
Alford, Colonel, 13
Alfred, Maine, 77, 83
American House, the; in Belfast, *135*;
   in Boston, 50, 114
Ames, Adelbert, 62, 65
Amisville, Virginia, 29
Anderson, Hugh J., 20, 198
Annapolis, 115–16, 124, 126, 129–31
Antietam, Battle of, 23, *24*, 25–26,
   27, 28–29, *30*, 36, 48
Appleton, John, *97*
Appomattox Court House, 143
Aquia Creek, 59
Armistead, Lewis, 69
Army of Northern Virginia: at Antie-
   tam, 25; becomes defensive, 70; at
   Bull Run, 22–23; cavalry division,
   49; commanded by Lee, 18; de-
   feated by Grant, 92; at Fredericks-
   burg, 57; invades Pennsylvania,
   61; loses Stuart, 107; at Marye's
   Height, 31, 34; mortally wounded,
   142; at the Rappahannock, 43; sur-
   renders, 144; takes the offensive,
   81
Army of Tennessee, 76, 92, 114, 125,
   144
Army of the Cumberland, 76, 92
Army of the James, 121
Army of the Ohio, 92
Army of the Potomac, 41, 77, 83,
   86–87, 129; Burnside commands
   the, 31; cavalry, 17, 29, 49–51, 107;
   at Chattanooga, 76; at Cold Harbor, 108; commanded by Meades,
   68; created by Little Mac, 13;
   deserters, 109; at Falmouth, 53;
   Frank Dickerson joins the, 14; at

the Grand Review, 158; Grant
   leads the, 92; Grant reviews the,
   106; on Lee's trail, 56; at Rappahannock River, 43; reinforced,
   121; at Richmond, 18; supplies
   carried to the, 119; triumphs at
   Gettysburg, 70; under Hooker's
   command, 55; weakened, 81;
   weapons handed over to the, 143;
   withdraws at Marye's Height, 34
Army of Virginia, 22
Aromatic belts, 21
Ash, Joseph P., 98, 100, 107–8, 178,
   198
Atlanta, Georgia, 92, 110, 115
Averell, William Woods, 44, 52, 54–
   55, 59, 198

Baden, James T., 198
Baltimore, 112, 114, 116, 120, 122, 126
Baltimore American, 93
Bangor, 160
Barnum's Hotel, 126
Barrington, Eliza, *185*. See also Eliza
   A. Dickerson.
Barrington, L.M., *185*
Barrows, William G., *97*
Batchelder, George, 148
Batchelder, Sarah Jane Hamlin, 148
Bealton, Station, 59
Belfast, Maine, 3, *4*, 70, 114, *127*, 161;
   the American House of, *135*; de-
   moralized by war, 129; Dickerson
   home in, *179*; fire of, 171–72, *173*;
   Grove Cemetery of, 186; and its
   involvement in the war, 71; J.Y.
   McClintock Block in, *38*; mayor
   of, 152; mourning of, 152; post
   office of, *21*; recruiting in, 72;
   soldiers from, 137–38; tense days
   in, 126; the Unitarian Church of,
   183, *184*
Belfast Democratic Association, 6

208